★**Gelman, Rita Golden.** Inside Nicaragua: young people's dreams and fears. 1988. 198p. illus. Watts, $13.90 (0-531-10538-5). **CH**

Nearly half of Nicaragua's population is under 15, and Gelman's warm, personal account of her eight-month stay there focuses on what it's like to be a teenager in a country at war. Unlike those writers who drop in to a new country for a few weeks and then feel qualified to write a book about it, Gelman lived with a family in Managua for seven months and traveled extensively to villages and rural areas. In a style both lively and intimate, she evokes the young peo:le's friendliness, humor, and sorrow. She speaks to the ardent revolutionary and the disaffected: soldiers (there's a compulsory two-year draft at age 17), peasants, commuters in the endless bus lines. Through personal interviews she integrates recent Nicaraguan history: a young woman tells of how she left her rich family at age 15 to join the guerrillas in the mountains and help overthrow the corrupt Somoza dictatorship. The most moving chapter describes the literacy crusade with its postrevolutionary fervor: a young man remembers his experience as one of 90,000 teenagers who spent five months in various parts of the country teaching adults and children to read. While Gelman makes it clear that her sympathy is with the Sandinistas and that she is bitterly ashamed of U.S. support for the contras, she is also candid about the problems, including severe shortages, official corruption, and mismanagement. The format is handsome and spacious, with a few photographs (one of a young mother carrying a baby and a gun), some footnotes, an annotated bibliography, and an index. Gr. 7–12. HR.

972.85 Nicaragua—Politics and government | Nicaragua—Social life and customs | Youth—Nicaragua [CIP] 87-33973

Booklist .7/88

INSIDE NICARAGUA

RITA GOLDEN GELMAN

"INSIDE NICARAGUA

YOUNG PEOPLE'S DREAMS AND FEARS"

Franklin Watts 1988
New York   London   Toronto   Sydney

Library of Congress Cataloging-in-Publication Data
Gelman, Rita Golden.
Inside Nicaragua : young people's dreams and fears/Rita Golden Gelman.
p. cm.
Bibliography: p.
Includes index.
Summary: The author describes her experiences traveling through Nicaragua and the
effects of the present conflict on the lives of the young people of this troubled country.
ISBN 0-531-15085-2. ISBN 0-531-10538-5 (lib. bdg.)
1. Nicaragua—Description and travel—1981—Juvenile literature. 2. Nicaragua—
Politics and government—1979—Juvenile literature. 3. Youth—Nicaragua—Attitudes—
Juvenile literature. 4. Nicaragua—Social life and customs—
Juvenile literature. [1. Nicaragua—Politics and government. 2. Nicaragua—
Social life and customs. 3. Youth—Nicaragua.] I. Title.
F1524.G45 1988 972.85—dc19   87-33973 CIP AC

For my mother and father, with love—
their example taught me to care,
and their love gave me the security
to do something about it

CONTENTS

INSIDE NICARAGUA

THE QUESTION

Oh, wait a minute," she says, when I tell her I have just returned from Nicaragua. "We studied those countries in my Spanish class. Is Nicaragua the one where the good government is fighting the bad guerrillas? Or is it the one where the bad government is fighting the good guerrillas?"

Depends who you ask.

1

ARRIVAL

It is *sweat-dripping hot when* we walk across the border from Honduras into Nicaragua. The Nicaraguan women who had been on my bus have towels or rags slung over their shoulders so they can soak up the sweat. I just drip, literally drip, as though someone is wringing out clothes on my head. From time to time, I wipe the sweat with the bottom of my shirt.

We walk down a hill into Nicaragua. Borders are always a disappointment to me. Going from one country into another should be more than just walking down a road. The color should change. You should go from green to orange like you do on a map. At the least you should be able to look off into the distance and see a line painted across the landscape.

But the only line is a ragged one of wet people, twenty-two Nicaraguans and two tourists. The Nicaraguans are returning from a shopping trip to El Salvador (the other country with either the good government and the bad guerrillas or the other way around). Honduras would be closer for the shoppers, but the Honduran government doesn't want Nicaraguans coming up for shopping sprees; so they go to El Salvador or Guatemala or Costa Rica, all of them also in Central America.

The men and women are carrying shopping bags, boxes, duffel bags, suitcases battered and new and filled with things that are hard to get in Nicaragua—things like toilet paper and toothpaste and deodorant, underwear, jeans, T-shirts, light bulbs, makeup, and toys.

The road is empty except for us and the Sandinista soldiers who are on top of every hill. The soldiers are looking not at us but off into the fields and hills surrounding us. They are looking for contras. The contras are a guerrilla army that, since 1979, when the Sandinistas won control of Nicaragua, has been trying to overthrow the new government.

The Sandinista soldiers are young, most of them still in their teens. They get drafted at the age of seventeen; but a lot of young men volunteer for the army before they are drafted—"to do my duty," "to get it over with," "to have an adventure," they tell me. One twelve-year-old soldier I meet tells me he joined "to get revenge": His father, mother, and little sister had been killed by the contras.

"It's dangerous along this road," says one of the women. She points out the abandoned customs office where government officials used to check passports and luggage. The building is shot up with bullet holes, and the ground around it is littered with empty sardine cans, old plastic bags, torn wrappers, and some mangled pieces of metal. The government had to move the office farther away from the border.

They had to move the people, too—the ones who used to live in the disintegrating shacks along the side of the road, the ones who used to farm the fields that stretch into the distance. Too close. Too dangerous. Good fertile land that used to feed people. Abandoned.

We come to a place on the road and everyone stops. We are to wait there for a ride to the new customs office. Some of the soldiers join us, guns slung over their shoulders, smiles on their faces. The people share snacks with them, exchange greetings.

These Sandinista soldiers are not scary soldiers like the kind I had seen in a little town in El Salvador, hiding behind sandbag walls, guns sticking through between the bags, pointing at the people in the street. These soldiers are friendly. I share my peanuts with two of them, and they ask me where I'm from and how long I'm planning to stay.

I am here in Nicaragua because of the battle between the Sandinistas and the contras. Ever since 1979, when Nicaragua had a revolution that brought the Sandinistas into power, Nicaragua has been a focal point of international tension. People and governments all over the world have taken sides in this conflict, and the different sides contradict each other. It's hard to know what to believe.

The front pages of newspapers in the United States are filled with stories about the problems in this Iowa-size, Spanish-speaking country with nearly three and a half million people. I have been to parties in the United States where people argue about which side is right.

"*They* are terrorists," says everyone. But for some, the "they" refers to the Sandinistas, and for others it refers to the contras.

I have come to Nicaragua to see for myself who the real villains are and to write a book about young people here, about what it's like to live in a country at war. By the time I finish my search for villains, I will have spent eight months in Nicaragua, traveled to fifteen of the sixteen *departmentos* (states), and talked to hundreds of Nicaraguans.

For now, as I stand in this road that has no cars, I tell the Sandinista soldiers that I am from the United States and that I am here as a tourist.

After about forty hot minutes, a pickup truck arrives, and we pile ourselves and our bags into the back for a fifteen-minute trip to the new customs area. It is beginning to cool off. The sun is low in the sky as we move past more abandoned shacks and barren fields.

Toward the end of the trip, we begin to see kids. Lots of them. Big ones, small ones. Small ones carrying even smaller ones. Kids pushing wheelbarrows with kids inside. Kids just hanging around, waving, staring. We are apparently in a safe zone—or at least an area where families can live.

The first step through the customs process is at a simple wooden stand, the kind where people might be selling sodas if the officials weren't inspecting passports and filling out forms. We line up. It is the first of thousands of lines I will stand in during my eight months in Nicaragua.

When it is my turn, the soldier inside the stand asks me for my passport. Then, looking at the information on the passport, he begins to fill out an entry card. Last name, first name, birthdate, nationality, passport number, and occupation. He looks up. The passport does not include occupation.

"What is your profession?" he asks in Spanish.

"Writer."

He smiles. The corners of his lips curl up into his mustache.

"Me too. I'm a writer too. I write poetry. What do you write?"

"Children's books."

"How nice. Do you have any with you?"

I look at the long line behind me as I fumble through my backpack. I pull out three books. He turns the pages of an easy-to-read book and smiles at the antics of a monkey who is trying to fly.

"Do you read English?" I ask.

"A little," he answers in English. Then he looks up. "I have a six-year-old daughter. May I take this home for her?"

I have experienced customs officials in other countries. Many of them want bribes just to pass you through. But I had been told that Nicaragua was different. Besides, I wasn't carrying these books to give them away to the first person I met.

"I brought the books to share with the children of Nicaragua," I say. "And I haven't even met any yet."

"Okay. No problem. I understand." And he finishes filling out my card. "Que le vaya bien"—May it go well for you, or, loosely, Have a good time.

And he passes me on to the other shacks and battered trailers for more questions and baggage inspection.

Twenty minutes later, I walk along a wooden-post fence that brings me back to the road. As I wait for the next pickup, I watch a group of soldiers behind one of the trailers. They are playing a tape of break-dance music, and two of them are dancing. Their guns are lying on the ground.

I don't notice the three boys and a girl who are approaching.

"Buenas tardes," they say. Good afternoon. There are four scruffy, barefoot kids looking up at me.

"Buenas tardes."

"What's your name?" asks the biggest.

When they hear my answer, they smile and nod to each other, as though they know something about me.

Then the big one speaks again. "Would you read us a book?"

And there, late in the day, on a nearly empty road in front of the customs office, perhaps observed by distant contras, I read them a book.

The next day I head for Managua, the capital city, two buses and hours of waiting away. There is a forty-five minute wait for the final bus—and a line with sixty-five people in it, not counting about twenty-five lap-sitting kids. The line keeps growing.

It is, of course, hot. And the busiest business in the dirt parking lot where the buses come in is the selling of uncarbonated, homemade fruit drinks called *frescas*.

"Fresca, fresca, fresca, fresca, fresca!" A ten-year-old girl in a torn, pink, ruffled dress is carrying a green plastic basin on her head. Her voice is harsh; her call, penetrating.

Another voice, this time a boy about eight, calls the flavors: "Mango, cacao! Fresca, fresca, fresca, fresca! Mango, mango, cacao!"

He is holding his orange plastic pail by its handle. Inside are dozens of sandwich-size plastic bags filled with colored liquid and ice. The tops are tied; there are no straws.

"Fresca, fresca, fresca, fresca!" I buy a brownish fresca from the girl, and she hands me a cold plop of a plastic bag with my drink inside. I watch the man in front of me to see how I'm supposed to drink it. He holds the bag, bites off one of the corners, and spits it out. Then he sort of squirts and sucks the fresca. I try it. It works.

The drink is sweet, cold, and wet. By the time the

bus comes, I've had three of them, and I'm an expert in biting off the corners of plastic bags.

There are also kids selling cut-up fruit in plastic bags and colored candies that look like popcorn balls. Other kids are selling newspapers, calling out the names of the papers: *"Barricada, Barricada, Barricaaaada! Barricada, Barricada, Barricaaaada!"*

"Barricada! Nuevo Diario! Barricada! Nuevo Diario!" The two newspaper sellers are boys, and each carries a stack of papers on his head.

There is a lot of movement when the bus pulls in. Everyone begins sorting packages, children, animals. When the door opens, the line—carefully maintained for nearly an hour—disintegrates completely. People push, shove, climb in windows. It is a four-hour bus ride to Managua, and everyone wants a seat.

One boy of about twelve is especially aggressive. He pushes his way through the crowd, practically stomping on the babies. It turns out that he is securing a seat for his pregnant seventeen-year-old sister, who wiggles her way through the crowd to sit in the seat he has saved. Once she is settled, he says good-bye and leaves.

The back door is pried open by several young men; dozens of people who were never even in line climb on ahead of people who have been waiting. On the roof, sacks of beans and corn and baskets of food or grain are piled up by the bus driver's assistant. The assistant, who is wearing a New York Mets shirt, lifts the huge bags onto his shoulders and climbs a vertical ladder to the roof.

There are also people on the roof—men and boys—twelve of them, tucked in among the sacks or riding on top of them. And a live goat, with its feet tied, and two turkeys.

The rest of us are inside the bus, pressed together like those potato chips that come in a can, every curve fitting into some other curve. The only problem is that people come in different sizes, and it isn't so neat. There are heads tucked under strangers' arms, waists into rear ends, fronts into backs, sides into fronts, and legs and feet and hands intertwined.

One half hour into the trip, my hand is on top of a nice-looking young man's on the overhead bar; I am kneeing someone else, and my head is pushing against a third stranger's shoulder. No one seems to be bothered by all this intimacy. In fact, it opens up communication. If you're holding hands with someone, can conversation be far behind?

A month later I will hear a joke going around Managua about the young wife of a soldier who called her mother one day: "Mom, guess what? You're going to be a grandmother."

"How wonderful," says the mother. "I didn't know Mario was home."

"He isn't," says the daughter. "I rode the bus yesterday."

So there we were, snuggled, twisted, and touching. The woman I am kneeing has offered to hold my backpack on her lap, along with her baby, who is playing with the straps and trying to unzip the zippers. The man in the seat next to her is holding the baby of the woman who is standing on my sneaker. And two soldiers are flirting with a pretty teenager in Sasson jeans. Or perhaps it's the other way around. Hard to tell: It's patriotic to flirt with a soldier. Suddenly the front of the bus bursts into song. I can't see, but I hear the voices of young girls, and the songs are a mixture of pop tunes and hymns from the Catholic church.

On top of all that, it's hot. But this time I'm carrying a towel over my shoulder. Most of the bodies in the bus are wet. I wonder why the bus doesn't smell of sweat, especially when you can't buy deodorant in Nicaragua.

The bus passes by fields of rice and onions, corn and sugarcane, swerving around huge holes in the road and avoiding gaping cracks in the pavement. We are on the main north-south highway.

"They're widening the roads in Nicaragua," goes the joke.

"Why?"

"To make room for more holes."

The houses we pass are small, many made of mud and stucco and painted two colors, light on the top—white or cream—and darker on the bottom—red, blue, green, or brown. They are all in need of painting. Other houses are made of sticks and boards and plastic bags.

The landscape is full of kids: sitting on doorsteps, climbing trees, pushing and riding in carts, galloping on stick horses, or riding—sometimes three of them at the same time—on real horses. We stop in a gas station and there are two kids in a barrel of water between the gas pumps, splashing and waving and giggling. Everywhere you go in Nicaragua, there are lots of kids. Nearly half the population is under fifteen.

We make a stop in an onion-growing town, and the bus is mobbed by kids selling onions with their green scallion leaves still attached.

"Onions, onions, onions, onions, onions!"

It's a contest. There's a kid at every other window of the bus, shouting and selling.

"Onions, onions, onions, onions!" Kids, seven, eight, and nine, hand over the onions and collect their money. They have to stand on tiptoe and reach up as high as they can while the passengers reach down.

We pull away five minutes later, leaving the kids counting their money and the bus smelling of onions.

2

MANAGUA

The dance floor is a lot like the bus, packed and sweaty. I had arrived in Managua two hours earlier, and my neighbors in the motel invited me to go dancing with them—live music under the stars.

The crowd is young and active; the music, a mix of American rock spiced with salsa and reggae. Teenagers as young as fourteen are drinking beer from plastic bags. You buy a beverage ticket at a booth and go to a stand to pick up your drink. There is no soda.

There are a lot of blue jeans and oversize shirts with hip belts on the girls and T-shirts with writing, mostly from the United States, on the guys: "Carey's

Hardware," "Detroit Tigers," "I may be crazy, but it keeps me from going insane," "Remember when air was clean and sex was dirty?" All the writing is in English.

It is 10:30 at night and still hot. People are wet with sweat, but no one seems bothered by it. The revolving mirrored balls and the flashing lights shine on an always-packed floor.

There is an excess of single guys, and the only way women can avoid dancing is to hide out far away from the dance floor. If you're anywhere near, several hands and smiles greet you wordlessly at the beginning of every new dance.

If there's a difference between the dancing here and the dancing back home, it's probably in the hips: more movement, more isolated hip gyrations here. Part of the reason is the Caribbean music. The east coast of Nicaragua is on the Caribbean, and hips are an important part of the Caribbean dance style. The east coast has influenced the bodies on this dance floor.

The group plays a dance called *Palo de Mayo*, "Maypole," which has everyone bumping and grinding in mock sex. The boys are freer with their movements than the girls, but everyone is very much into the sensuousness of the dance.

Now the group is playing "Lonely is the Night" and singing in accented English.

"Where are you from?" asks Carlos, the young man who has asked me to dance.

"What?" I can't hear him; the music is loud.

"Where are you from?" he shouts.

"The United States," I shout back.

"How long have you been here?"

"I arrived three hours ago!" We are still shouting.

"Tomorrow," he yells at me, "I am taking you to Xiloá!" A nearby lake.

Nicaraguans are not shy.

Four of us take off at noon the next day on the bus. I bring a friend from the motel, and Carlos brings his seven-year-old sister. Two hot, overcrowded, sweaty buses later, the beach is no longer a luxury; it's a necessity.

We get off at a lake just a few miles outside Managua. Carlos answers my questions as we walk to the shore. He is wearing a navy T-shirt with the short sleeves rolled up. His hair is long and curly. His eyes are brown with a touch of green. He is a medical student in his second year.

"In the days of Somoza, I could never have thought about becoming a doctor. The university was for rich people. Now it's free." (Somoza was the corrupt dictator of Nicaragua. His family ruled Nicaragua for forty-three years. He was thrown out by the revolution in 1979.)

As we approach the lake, we walk along a grassy slope that leads down toward the sand. The grass is spotted with picturesque thatched roofs on poles, with benches underneath—protection from the tropical sun. We pass bars and restaurants with tables outside. The area has the look of a resort hotel.

"All this," Carlos sweeps his hand around the lake, "used to be their playground. Somoza and his friends. There was a private club over there," he points. "It's public now."

A pickup has just driven up to one of the shaded huts. There are eight kids in the back and coolers and blankets and towels and a skinny dog. And a radio playing Madonna. Four adults and two babies climb out of the cabin.

"That family would never have been here if Somoza was still in power," says Carlos, pointing to the new arrivals. "Resort-type places were for the rich."

"Come on. Let's go in the water," says Carlos's sister, getting back to more important things. And we race across the burning sand to the cool water of the once off-limits lake.

I spend the next day sitting in a rocking chair visiting with Carlos's family. Finding his house was an adventure.

People in Managua don't live at number-name addresses like 25 Main Street. Most of the streets don't have names, and most of the houses don't have numbers. A typical Managua address goes something like:

Carlos García
From the Larreynaga Bridge, two blocks toward the lake, one block up, twelve yards on the right-hand side, second house.
Managua.

My favorite addresses of all are the ones that start with something that isn't there any more: "From where the hospital used to be, two blocks down. . . ."

Carlos's mother, Gabriela, is a warm, friendly woman in her fifties who loves to reminisce. She talks about the old days all afternoon. Then she cooks supper: a rice-bean combination, fried eggs, boiled green bananas, and tortillas.

Gabriela tells me that they eat meat twice a week, and Sunday isn't a meat day.

At seven on a Monday morning, the streets of Managua are filled with children, most of them dressed in blue pants or skirts and white tops, ironed and spotless. Even in poor neighborhoods—where people live in houses made of wood and plastic and rusty metal 7-Up signs, where the floors are dirt and the water is out back—even there, the kids are clean when they go to school. And their hair is wet from washing.

At seven on almost any morning, the homeowners in the neighborhood where I am staying are already outside, sweeping the dry leaves and trash from the street in front of their houses.

The brooms are made of dozens of firm branches from some bush, hand-tied together and then to a pole. It's a perfect design for the paving stones of the streets. The uneven ends get into the cracks.

At least once a week a man carrying about twelve brooms on his shoulder walks through the streets of this neighborhood calling, "Escooobas, escooobas!" Broooooms, brooooooms!

Once the leaves are swept up into a pile, the sweeper sprinkles some gasoline on them and lights a fire. In the early mornings in my neighborhood there is always the smell of smoke.

If they could, the homeowners would also be hosing down the street, especially if it is unpaved. The water keeps the dust from getting into everything. In the dry season, dust is part of life. It grits as you eat your food; it coats your nose as you breathe; and it is constantly blamed for colds, coughs, and sneezes.

But it's Monday, and they can't hose the street. They can't even take a shower or get a drink of water from the tap. On Monday and Thursday in this neighborhood, there is no water from about five in the morning until after eleven at night, because of a combination of pump problems and overpopulation. Rich, poor, it doesn't matter. If you are one of the million or so people who live in Managua, you don't have any water two days a week. What you do is fill up pails and pots, barrels and sinks and bottles the night before. Some women get up in the middle of the night to do the laundry.

On my first Monday morning in Managua, I brush my teeth without water and leave for a look at the city. The bus stop is packed. Clean, ironed, crisp-looking workers and students, waiting. Plaid shirts, jeans, colorful skirts and pants, tops in pink and blue and white.

Two buses pass without stopping. There are three people hanging out the front door of the second bus; one is holding on to the mirror. The following week the paper will report two people killed when the mirrors they were hanging onto pulled out of their rusty moorings.

We have been waiting for more than half an hour when finally a bus stops and about twenty of us cram on. Once on, I begin to push my way through to the back. City buses are different from the buses that go between cities. The trick on city buses is not to find a comfortable position for the long trip but rather to squeeze through the packed crowd so that you can be at the rear exit when you reach your stop.

I get off near the Plaza of the Revolution. Gabriela had suggested I begin my tour there, where downtown Managua *used to be*. Managua no longer has a downtown, just empty lots with weeds growing on them, green weeds in the rainy season and brown weeds in the dry months. This Monday morning in May, the fields—where once there were stores and high-rise buildings and restaurants and offices—are brown and dry and dusty.

From time to time there is the shell of a building, twisted steel girders embedded in the concrete remains of walls, remnants of the downtown that used to be. The destruction of downtown Managua did not occur in the war that is going on now nor did it happen during the revolution in 1979. Downtown Managua was destroyed in the earthquake of 1972.

In the Plaza of the Revolution, there is what looks like a grand cathedral; but on closer look, the cathedral turns out to be a shell. The side and back walls have crumbled; there is no roof. And inside, shriveled brown weeds have replaced the people who once prayed there.

The empty lots, the mangled remains of buildings, the facade of the cathedral are permanent reminders of an earthquake that swallowed the city and more than fifteen thousand of its inhabitants.

Gabriela had talked about the earthquake. She had been downtown that Friday afternoon in 1972, buying Christmas presents for Carlos and the family. The stores were crowded. There were the usual Christmas sales. Last-minute shoppers were rushing around in pre-Christmas madness. The streets were draped with lights and Santa Clauses and silver and green and red decorations. Some of the taller buildings were decorated too, but those buildings were most impressive at night with their lights in the shape of Christmas trees reaching into the sky.

When she arrived home from shopping, Gabriela sat down to wrap the gifts and think about Christmas dinner. It was December 22, and at midnight on December 24, the traditional Christmas meal would be served, and the "God Child" would leave presents for the children. Already the meal was planned and many of the ingredients were on the shelf—olives and capers and raisins for the stuffing, rum for the cake.

Gabriela felt uneasy as she wrapped. So uneasy that she went to the phone and called one of her older children. "Is everything all right? I have this feeling that something's wrong," she said.

"Oh, Mom, stop worrying. Everything's fine."

"Well, be careful," she said.

"Sure, I will. Don't worry," he said, placating her.

Still, after her family went to sleep for the night, she got up and unlocked the door, leaving it slightly open, just in case they needed a quick exit.

"I felt stupid doing it," she tells me, "when I had no

reason to suspect anything. But I did it anyway, without telling anyone."

At 12:30 in the morning, Managua began to shake. With an unimaginable fury, the earth convulsed. It rocked and rumbled and heaved.

"It was as though we were in a boat being tossed around by rolling ocean waves, except it was the solid earth that was tossing us, an earth that was no longer solid," says Gabriela. "And the sound was terrifying, like thousands of bombs exploding at once."

In just a few minutes, Managua, its houses, its factories, its few high-rise buildings, and its people were buried in rubble.

Gabriela felt the first tremor and charged out of bed just before a beam crushed the bed to the floor. As she raced through the house collecting her five children, the glass ceiling fixture crashed. They ran out the door, cutting their feet on the broken glass, leaving bloody footprints on the tiles. Then they watched in terror as the house crumbled. And they stood, clinging to each other, as the earth shook beneath their feet.

The days that followed were spent digging out bodies. Parents were searching the rubble for children; children were looking for parents under piles of rock and plaster and roof beams. And people were standing in line at the cemetery, participating in mass burials. There were not enough coffins, so the dead were wrapped in paper or sheets or whatever could be found. As the days went by thousands of unclaimed corpses began to decay; many were burned in huge funeral pyres to stop the spread of disease.

And the streets were filled with looters. People abandoned their homes and other people looted them. Gabriela tells the story of a family that after two days of digging finally uncovered Grandmother's body from the rubble of her house. They also found a big free-standing closet and decided to store Grandma in the closet while they went off to get a truck. When they got back, the closet, with Grandma inside, had been stolen.

"Imagine their faces when they opened it up!" Gabriela says, smiling with tears in her eyes.

In the days following the earthquake, Managua was in shock. People talked about the end of the world, about Sodom and Gomorrah, about Judgment Day. They walked through the streets reading the Bible, fingering rosary beads, praying, moaning, crying. Crying for the dead, crying for their city that was no more.

The earthquake was the beginning of tumultuous years in Nicaragua. Until the earthquake the world knew little about the country except the words of a popular song that ironically began, "Managua, Nicaragua, is a beautiful town." As news of the tragedy spread, international aid poured in: food, medicines, millions of dollars. But as the aid poured in, corruption flourished. The army, known as the Guardia, looted stores while keeping the people away at gunpoint. Some Guardia, put in charge of keeping looters out, willingly accepted bribes to let them in.

"Guardia families went into business and became rich," Gabriela tells me. "They would unload the medicines at the airport, the stuff that was coming in as gifts from all over the world; and then they would set up pharmacies and sell them. I knew one woman, the wife of a Guardia officer, who sold medicines out of her garage. The people would go to the hospitals and there would be no medicine. Or else the Guardia would confiscate donations of food and blankets and other things and sell them to the homeless who were living in tent cities. Who had money in those days? We were happy to have our lives."

◢

Anastasio Somoza, dictator of Nicaragua from 1967 until his overthrow in 1979, used the tragedy to increase his personal wealth. He knew the country would need building materials, so he went into the building material business. The roads would need paving; he went into the manufacture of paving stones. The people would need land for housing projects; so he bought land cheap and sold it to his own government at tremendous profits. He knew that the homeless people, who were moving into the new settlements on the outskirts of the city, would need buses to get into Managua. He and his friends and family went into the bus business.

Somoza had an inside track on what would be needed, and he took full advantage of what he knew. While the people suffered, Somoza stockpiled money, and he and his cronies came out of the earthquake millions and millions of dollars richer.

Challenged by a foreign reporter about the ethics of his maneuvering, Somoza is said to have replied, "I'm just a businessman trying to do a little business."

After the earthquake, nearly 80 percent of the buildings in Managua were uninhabitable; the whole city was bulldozed.

Today, there is still no downtown: It was never rebuilt. But the neighborhoods were; and Managua, with more than a million inhabitants, remains the hub of the country. There are other smaller cities in Nicaragua, but the majority of the people live in villages and on farms and in mountain huts far from paved roads and plumbing.

Nicaragua, the biggest of the five Central American countries, is a country rich with agricultural lands, minerals, and timber. It has beautiful lakes and massive volcanic mountains, the Atlantic Ocean on one side, the Pacific on the other.

The Spanish colonized Nicaragua, and during the three hundred years that they ruled the country, they introduced their language, their customs, their Catholic religion. Ever since Nicaragua won its independence from Spain in 1821, up until the present, its history has been violent; there were dictators and civil wars and interventions by outside countries. The most recent dictators, the Somoza family, who ruled Nicaragua from 1936 until 1979, were thrown out by a revolution. Now the people who made that revolution are trying to change the course of Nicaraguan history; the contras are trying to stop them; and I am here to witness firsthand what is going on.

On my second day in Managua, I spend the morning in the plaza, visiting the tomb of a revolutionary hero, eating a tortilla stuffed with marinated beef and topped with cabbage salad, and wandering inside the massively columned National Palace. People are standing in long lines, waiting to pay city fees or to get special stamps and papers they need for various transactions. Later in my stay I will find myself in line to buy the stamps and tickets that I need in order to get permission to stay longer than a month in the country. The line is ten people long, and each person seems to take forever. Finally my turn arrives. When I ask for my ticket, the man hears my accent.

"North American?" he asks.

I nod.

"How long have you been here? How do you like it? Are you working here?"

His questions have nothing to do with the tickets. He feels like chatting with me and isn't at all bothered by the long line. Nor was the soldier at the border. Nor was the mechanic when I asked him directions this morning. He was fixing a car. He stopped his work and walked me to the corner so he could point to the house I was looking for.

Business in Nicaragua is different from business as I know it at home. Here it is filtered through the natural warmth and friendliness of most Nicaraguans. One day I meet a Nicaraguan man who has recently returned from working a year in Miami.

"How was it?" I ask him.

"I earned a lot of money," he says. "But I really didn't like it. I felt like a machine. I had to be places at an exact time. Work without talking. Watch the clock for my breaks. That's not how I want to live. It's dehumanizing."

3

THE NEIGHBORHOODS

The next day I decide to visit some of the neighborhoods in Managua, but I can't figure out how to do it. The city is too big, and it is too hot to walk from end to end; buses are impossible; and you can't just get in a cab and say, "Give me a tour of Managua."

The cabs, nearly all of them held together with wire and string, take five people at a time and as many kids and babies as will fit. The driver tries to find five people who are going more or less along the same route. You wave him over. If you're lucky, he stops, and you call out your destination. Most of the time he shakes his head no and moves on without you.

Finally I decide to walk. The first thing I notice is that Managua is filled with uniformed soldiers. Like the border guards, they are young. And friendly.

I walk down a street that is lined with government buildings and stop to watch three soldiers who are guarding one of the buildings. The building itself is an old mansion, once the home of a rich family; most of the wealthy Nicaraguans abandoned their homes and left the country when Somoza was overthrown. There is a huge mango tree in the front yard, heavy with ripe green mangoes. The soldiers, who have tossed their guns on the lawn, are all throwing sticks at the mangoes, trying to knock down some snacks.

I walk through one neighborhood filled with houses that might be found in any U.S. suburb—one-story ranches with lawns and flowering shrubs. Then I walk through another neighborhood of dirt roads and shacks.

I stop to watch a bunch of kids playing baseball. They are using a stick for a bat. I cannot figure out what the ball is made from, but it is navy blue. Baseball is the number one sport in Nicaragua.

As I watch the game, a boy about eight comes by carrying three plastic bags filled with milk.

"Doña Rosa has milk," he calls to the players.

And the game breaks up while the kids race to their houses to tell their mothers and to get money.

Doña Rosa has a little store just down the block. Like most of the neighborhood stores, it is in what was once the front room of a house. There is no sign outside; but the line, mostly of kids with pails or sacks to carry the plastic bags in, is already about twenty-five people long, so I know I'm in the right place.

"I never know when I'm going to get milk," Doña Rosa tells me. "Sometimes two weeks go by and they don't bring me any."

I ask the kids what it is like not having enough milk. They compete to tell me their stories.

"Only the baby can have milk in my house, and it's usually the powdered stuff, but sometimes we can't get that, and my mother says he could die if he doesn't have milk," says a little girl with braids on top of her head, a baby in her arms and a cloth sack over her shoulder.

"Yeah, well, my baby sister *did* die."

"Because she didn't have milk?"

"No. But she died," says a boy of about seven wearing a Snoopy shirt that is hanging off one shoulder.

"Well, my brother died in the war." This boy is carrying the ball from the baseball game.

"Can I see the ball?" I ask.

"Sure. My grandmother helped me make it."

The outer layer of the ball is a man's sock, tightly wrapped and wrapped around itself and then sewn together around the edges. Inside, he tells me, is a rock and a bunch of rags that they kept wrapping around until they had a baseball-size ball.

Everything is hard to get in Nicaragua.

Soon it is seven o'clock in the evening. The sun has gone down. The heat remains. The neighborhood in which I am walking is middle class, with houses that have refrigerators and tile floors and more than one room. As I walk in the street, I discover that the same music is coming out of every house that I pass. Then the same voices.

From seven to eight in the evening, wherever you are in Nicaragua, everyone is watching the *novela*, the soap opera. And when the houses are hot and the heat is trapped inside, people bring their chairs, most of them wooden rockers, outside, face them in, and view the novela from outside.

Government officials have been known to adjourn meetings early so they could catch the novela. And children, even babies, soon come to know that the usual indulgences they receive from their mothers or grandmothers are on hold from seven to eight. Wet diapers stay wet. Glasses of water are brought later. The best the kids can hope for is to be held and rocked in front of the TV. All over Nicaragua, evening meetings are held after eight. And when a fictitious doctor was the star of one soap, there was no surgery scheduled in one of the largest hospitals in Managua for that hour. The real doctors wanted to watch.

On this street something interesting happens after the novela is over. People turn their rockers to face the street. Neighbors greet each other. The kids go back to playing. And those people who feel like walking can catch up on the neighborhood gossip—or spread it.

As I turn a corner on this, my fourth night in Managua, I notice a crowd in front of one of the houses. Benches. Chairs. People sitting; people standing. I move closer and see that inside the front room is a coffin, backed by a ceiling-to-floor lacy white curtain and surrounded by flowers—in vases, in jars, in cans that once contained powdered milk. Flanking the coffin are two giant wreaths standing five feet high. One is from Daniel Ortega, the president of Nicaragua. I speak to some people at the edge of the crowd.

"Come in," says a woman, leading me by the elbow into the house. She points to the mother. Then to the girlfriend.

"Francisco was eighteen. We were planning his welcome-home party," she tells me. "He only had two more weeks left in the army."

I look into the open coffin at the face of a young man who should be at a disco or snuggling somewhere with the pretty girl who is sitting in front of me. The red-and-black flag of the Sandinistas is draped over the bottom half of the coffin. It is the symbol of the revolutionary government of Nicaragua. Francisco died yesterday morning serving that revolution. A contra mine blew up the Toyota Land Cruiser he was driving.

The mother brings me a cup of coffee. I hug her wordlessly and sit down. The woman who led me into the house sits next to me. She points to a young man in the other room.

"That's his brother. He's sixteen. Next year it's his turn."

The brother is drunk.

It is 5:30 in the morning and the biggest market in Managua is swirling with color. There are huge piles of bananas, green ones, yellow ones, giant ones, miniatures. And onions with their green tails sticking out. And baskets of oranges and tangerines and brown roots (yucca) that look like long, skinny sweet potatoes. There are red and green peppers and aisles of tomatoes. Cabbages, watermelon slices, mangoes, papayas.

And people, moving in and out of aisles, carrying sacks on their shoulders, baskets on their heads, pushing carts down alleys that are too small and screaming, screaming, "Watch out!" And you'd better.

The people are swirls themselves, all colors, moving up and down and in and out of the streets and aisles. In their reds and blues and yellows and pinks, they are piling the fruit, sorting the sizes, hawking their wares to each other:

"Plastic bags, plastic bags! All sizes!" shouts one.

"Paper, paper, paper!" shouts another.

They're selling banana leaves to the people who cook and ice to the people who sell drinks.

In some corners there is the smell of rotting fruit; in others, the rich aroma of meat grilling over coals or corn roasting or coffee, steaming up from huge pots where women ladle it out into plastic cups and you stand there and drink it and return the cup. There is no milk for the coffee, and the sugar is added to the pot because everyone in Nicaragua puts sugar in coffee.

In the Mercado Oriental (Eastern Market), you can buy meat and fish and beans and rice and sugar and powdered milk—even when there are none to be found in the rest of the city. And you can also buy deodorant and shampoo and toilet paper and ketchup and bubble gum. But most of this merchandise is black market—and illegal. And most Nicaraguans can't afford the prices. Goods here are sometimes five times more than the normal price; a can of powdered milk can cost more than a week's salary. For years the government has been trying to find a way to crush the black market. And can't. Where there's scarcity, there's usually a black market.

But the Mercado Oriental is more than a black market. It's people. And especially kids. At six in the morning the place is crowded with kids. Babies swinging in hammocks. Four-year-olds sorting fruit. Seven-year-olds selling coffee. And there are the roving sellers: kids with containers of candies, pastries, tortillas on their heads, calling out their wares.

Toward late morning, a woman stops me as I walk past her stand. She is stirring a stew of tomatoes, onions, meat, and spices. Next to the pot she is stirring is another filled with the dish I had had at Carlos's house: beans and rice together with a touch of onion and garlic. It's called *gallo pinto*. And next to her fire stove are a table and two picnic benches. A man is sitting at one, eating some stew; a boy about ten is eating gallo pinto at the other.

I ask the woman about the children who hang out in the market. I had heard that there were kids who lived here among the stalls, who slept and ate and stole in the Mercado Oriental. She talks as she stirs the stew, her forehead dripping in the heat of the day and the pot.

"You're interested in kids? I'll bet there are five hundred kids who sleep here every night and beg for their food. We all give them a meal now and then. And so do the customers. See that man over there?" She points to the man at the picnic table. "He bought the gallo pinto for that kid. And take a good look at those two."

She points to two kids who must be about five and seven. They are making their way among the stalls, barefoot, wearing rags.

"Their parents are drunks. They all live here, here in the market. The kids sniff glue; you can see it in their eyes. They're drugged most of the time."

There is a young man standing at the counter near the woman. He is carefully cutting off the thin rind of an orange and leaving the white cushiony part intact. On the street they sell oranges this way. First the orange skin is cut away; then they slice about a half an inch off the top and hand it to you. The white part is like a natural cup. You eat the orange by squeezing, sucking, and spitting out the seeds. When the juice is gone, you throw away the "cup." The young man is making himself a snack.

"He's my son," says the woman. She introduces us.

Isidro is fourteen and big, both wide and high.

"Are you here every day?" I ask him.

"My brother and I alternate," he says. "One of us is always here with her, and the other is at home with the little kids; they're four, six, and ten. On my day, I get up with my mother at three in the morning. We catch the bus at four to come into Managua, and we're here by five. I help her in a lot of different ways. I buy vegetables and meat. I carry stuff. I help her sell, and I wash dishes, and I bring her water from the communal spout. I don't do any cooking, but I cut things up and help in the preparation. And I help get the fires going and things like that."

"You can't run a place like this with just one person," says his mother. "I need their help."

Isidro continues. "At home I clean the house, wash clothes, mop, sweep, and take care of the kids. I like giving them baths and keeping track of them. It's a lot easier now than when they were babies. There are no diapers to wash and change all day long. Just the usual dirty clothes."

Isidro is asked to get some ice. While he is gone, a twelve-year-old boy walks by selling shelled peanuts. "Maní, maní, maní!" Peanuts, peanuts, peanuts! There are a lot of kids who sell peanuts. They sell them on the streets, on the buses, at the bus stops to the people waiting in line, in bars at night. They buy the nuts at the beginning of the day in a giant bag, and then they repackage them into tiny plastic bags.

"That one works for a living," says the woman, "but he's a delinquent. During the day, he beats up the little kids, and who knows what he does at night."

Isidro returns with a huge hunk of ice on his shoulder.

"How old were you when you left school?" I ask.

"I didn't leave," he answers. "I still go to school. We get home from the market at around four o'clock. I bathe and get ready and leave for school at five-thirty. I get out at nine."

I ask him what he thought about the revolution, about the Sandinista government. Had his life changed any?

He shakes his head. "I don't think about it much."

"And what about military service? Do you think about that."

"Not really," he answers. "Mostly I just think about going to sleep."

4

THE RIVERA FAMILY

The first time I meet the Rivera kids, the older brothers are rolling the three-year-old. They have curved him into an old truck tire they found and are rolling the tire with him inside.

There is a moment of suspense when the rolling stops and everyone waits anxiously to see what condition Chele will be in. He wiggles out, unable to walk, and lies in the middle of the tire. Then he utters his first words, "Otra vez." Again. And everyone starts screaming for turns.

When there are seven kids in the family and five cousins next door, there's always someone to roll—and someone to do the rolling.

The Rivera kids, including the cousins, are aged fourteen, thirteen, twelve, nine, seven, six, five, four, three, two, two, and two. I live with them for seven months.

One afternoon we are sitting on Grandma's porch.

"Take the string," says Rosa, one of the cousins, who is twelve. She is holding an imaginary string between her thumb and forefinger. I take it.

"Stretch it out." I do.

"Wrap it around your ear." I take the imaginary string and roll it around my ear.

"You're crazy," she says.

Not to be outdone by his cousin, seven-year-old Carlos says to me, "Say 'ding.' "

"Ding."

"Dong," he replies, bopping me on the head.

"Copo mopo sepe llapa mapa upu steped?"

Ramón, the fourteen-year-old, has asked me a question in some weird language. It isn't Spanish.

"Say it again."

"Copo mopo sepe llapa mapa upu steped?"

Suddenly I get a flash. It's like the languages kids in the United States use when they don't want the adults to understand. They break up words and add something in the middle. For example, "What is your name?" is "**Whi**dig**at** i**dig**i**s** y**idig**our** n**idig**ame?"

Ramón is doing something similar in Spanish. I finally figure out that he is asking me my name. The Spanish is *Cómo se llama usted?* He's separating the syllables, throwing in a *p*, and repeating the vowel. It ends up "Copo mopo" for *cómo* and "llapa mapa" for *llama*.

I answer, "Mepe llapa mopo Ripi Tapa." *Me llamo Rita.*

"How did you know that?" he says. I had passed his test.

▰

One morning, shortly after I arrive, I wake up to the hysterical crying of a baby. Sobbing, wailing, screaming, moaning for "Mama, mama, mama," and wailing again. It is obvious that no one is attending to this child. I turn on the radio but it doesn't drown the screaming. I wash, get dressed, and try to read something. Still the child is screaming. Now there is a second voice, also crying uncontrollably and endlessly.

Finally I give up trying to stay out of it and leave my room, which is a few feet from the house. I am nervous as I follow the sound. And then I see them. Two big green parrots, singing the songs they had learned from the babies.

"They can do all the kids," says Ramón, who joins me at the cage. "The high-pitched cry with the squeak is Angela, the one with the 'Mama, mama, mama' is Verónica, and the straight screaming is Juan Carlos having a temper tantrum."

Ramón, who at fourteen looks like he could be a candidate for Menudo, the singing group, has soft, bedroomy eyes; wavy, long dark hair; and a languid, sensuous walk. He is wearing a black T-shirt, short sleeves rolled up to the shoulders. On it, Snoopy is saying in English, "I'm not perfect, but pretty perfect."

Ramón is shy and quiet, but he clearly knows that he's good-looking. He once told me he'd had around fourteen girlfriends: "Silvia, Elena, Daisy, Adolfina—" he paused. "I can't remember the others."

Ramón is the oldest of all the kids; he was born three months after the earthquake, when his father was sixteen years old and his mother had just turned fifteen. He is standing at the parrot cage holding his almost-two-year-old sister in his arms. His big white-and-brown dog, Gormío, is wandering nearby; his father, Marco, is about fifty feet away, working on his taxi. Marco is a cab driver.

"Ramón," Marco booms as though Ramón is miles away.

Ramón doesn't react.

"Ramón, come here!"

"He wants me to help him," Ramón tells me. "I don't like working on cars. Besides, he's mad at me because I didn't sweep and mop the house yesterday." He waits a few minutes more before he puts the baby down and walks over. Gormío follows him. So does Franci, the baby.

Marco needs a tool from the house. Ramón walks toward his house, slowly, trailed by the dog, the baby, and me. We pass by a mango tree.

"Buenos días!" Good morning! calls a voice from the tree.

I look up. There are four kids looking down at me. A mango drops at my feet.

"He always says I don't do anything around the house," continues Ramón, "but it seems to me that I'm always doing stuff. Practically every minute they're asking me to do something else."

We are walking across a dirt path that leads from his grandmother's house to Ramón's house about fifty yards away. Ramón's great-grandmother is standing at the outdoor sink in front of his house, washing clothes. As we approach she walks from the sink to the clothesline. She has a problem with her legs, and when she walks, she waddles like a duck, going from one spread-out leg to the other. The baby falls into line behind her, waddling like a duck in imitation.

"Look at Franci!" calls Ramón, laughing.

His mother and three kids come out to look. Everyone laughs, including Great-grandma. The other three kids fall into line. Now there are four of them waddling behind her.

Ramón gets the tool and is soon under the car, tightening a bolt. Marco is greasing the totally disassembled steering system, from the steering wheel to the tires. His cab, like most of those in Managua, is something of a wreck. The right front fender doesn't exist; you can see the shock absorbers. Nor does the grille; the front of the hood sticks out beyond the lights like a big upper lip. The left front fender is badly dented. And the once-yellow paint gives the cab the look of a car that is about to go in for a paint job. The hood and the trunk are held closed with wire. Inside, the door panels are missing, and in order to open the right front door, you have to tangle with a mess of wires.

Car parts are hard to get and very expensive. Nicaragua does not manufacture them, so they have to be imported by the government and paid for in dollars, the currency of the international market. Nicaragua doesn't have enough dollars to take care of its needs and Nicaraguan money is worthless outside of Nicaragua.

When Marco needed a carburetor last week, he had to stand in line at the distribution store all night long so he'd have a chance when the place opened in the morning. At 10 A.M., he finally reached the front and they were out of carburetors.

"Ramón!" calls his grandmother from the porch of her house. "We have to go."

Ramón climbs out from under the car. He has to help her bring "the provisions." Like almost everything else, food is scarce too. The government has set up neighborhood distribution places for basic items like rice, beans, sugar, cooking oil, and soap. After standing in a long line, each family is allowed to purchase a certain amount every fifteen days. They have a card that gets stamped when they've picked up their allotment. Supermarkets offer empty shelves, lots of cleaning supplies, and nonessentials like Worcestershire sauce, vinegar, and mustard.

Ramón and his grandmother leave with a wagon. An hour and a half later (the store is on the next block), they return without the sugar, which never arrived. They have to go back the next day. When the two of them walk into the yard, they are greeted by a percussion band. Eight kids are sitting under the mango tree, banging on things. They are playing empty cans, pieces of metal, a pail, a pot, and a rusty fender. The drumsticks are sticks and boards and old broom handles. Carlos, the seven-year-old, is conducting.

Grandma and Ramón bring the provisions into the house and return to join the audience. The kids are ecstatic, playing to a rapt crowd.

A week or two later, Ramón and I are sitting in rocking chairs on the porch of his grandmother's house. It is a long porch about thirty feet long by ten feet wide. Ramón's teacher is sick, so he has no school.

We are eating oranges from a huge pile that a cousin brought from the country. The oranges are mounded up, about a thousand of them, in the corner of the porch. The peak of the pile is about three feet off the ground.

As we talk, background noise is provided by Juan Carlos, Ramón's two-year-old cousin, who is pushing an old metal TV table from one end of the porch to the other, then back again.

Ramón and I are translating an American rock song into Spanish. Ramón is sitting with a borrowed tape recorder on his lap, and we keep playing the song over and over again while I write the English and Ramón writes the Spanish translation. Ramón has spent the whole day at his grandmother's because he is avoiding his father. They have had another fight.

"I didn't wash my clothes," he says. "I started and then left them in the sink. So my dad got real mad and he started to push me around with the excuse that he has to discipline me so I can become a better, more responsible person. When somebody my age is treated like that, he's bound to get annoyed. So when that happens, I stop talking to him and I won't answer his questions. Then he punishes me more. He doesn't let me go out with my friends, and he gives me lots of errands to do. It's not easy, but I guess you have to learn to get along with your parents. I'm having a hard time."

Juan Carlos interrupts us. He has taken the cloth cover off his grandmother's sewing machine, put it over his head, and is now walking around like a ghost. Ramón picks him up, gives him a twirl, and puts him down with a hug. We go back to the music.

"Most of all I like disco music," he tells me. "I especially like Chicago and Michael Jackson, but I like romantic stuff, too, and salsa and break-dance. We always have music at our parties and a lot of dancing. If you have a girlfriend, you have to watch out at parties. Like sometimes a guy will touch your girlfriend just to annoy you, and then maybe there's a fight between the two guys. What usually happens in the end is that the girl is so disgusted by the fighting that she breaks up with you, even if you didn't start it."

"Tell me a little about girls and dating in Nicaragua."

He likes the question . . . and the topic.

"I like girls who are pretty and good students and responsible. And I like to find out about their families, too, I mean how they feel about us going out. Sometimes if the family doesn't like you, or if they don't like the idea that their daughter has a boyfriend, they can treat you badly.

"When I have a girlfriend, I try to be interested in her problems, like how she's getting along with her parents and if she's happy with me, and how she feels generally. I think part of a relationship is telling the other person if she or he does something wrong. You should be able to say, 'Oh, don't be like that.' Everybody can always improve.

"Sometimes if two people are in love, they have sexual relations, and then the girl gets pregnant and they get married and have a pretty boring life. They can't go out any more because they have to take care of the baby. They don't go to movies or parties or discos. And when they do go out, they have to take the baby. Suppose the baby cries. It can ruin everything."

I think about the fact that Ramón's parents were fifteen and sixteen when Ramón was born.

I ask him if he's thought about his future, about what he'd like to do.

"Whatever I choose, I know I'll have to work hard and study hard. Maybe I'll leave the country and study abroad. I really don't know what my future will be. I have to think about military service."

At seventeen Ramón will have to go into the army for two years.

"I think about it a lot," he tells me. "I spent three months in the militia last year. That's not the army; anybody can join. They give you training, but they don't send you out to fight. They gave us guns and we shot at some wooden boards. I liked using the gun, but only like that, for fun. I'm not interested in getting killed or killing anybody. My father wants me to go in the army. He says we have to fight to protect our country, and he says it'll make a man out of me. He and my mother fight about that a lot. She wants me to leave the country so I don't have to go."

Juan Carlos, this time pushing a chair, passes by. He has been joined by his cousin, Angela, who is kicking a can. Ramón leans over and gives Juan Carlos a kiss and Angela a pat. Juan Carlos kicks Angela. She picks up her can and runs inside, crying.

"I'd like to be a doctor or an engineer," says Ramón, finishing his answer to my question. "I want to help people, to help my country advance. I don't want to fight."

Our conversation is interrupted by Rosa, Ramón's twelve-year-old cousin, who has just returned from school.

"How was it?" I ask her.

"Horrible," she says. I ask her why.

"Because of Luis. He's a creep."

"What does he do?"

"Everything. He steals our notebooks and hides our shoes, and he has horrible nicknames that he calls everyone. Like, for example, he calls me 'Mafalda.'"

Mafalda is a fat, funny-looking cartoon character on television and in the comics. Rosa is chubby.

"And he calls one girl 'Little Turkey' and another 'Cat Face' and another 'Shoes,' because once she wore an ugly pair of shoes. And one of my friends has these big eyes that stick out. He calls her 'Crab.' Another one has a big nose and he calls her 'Machete.' [A machete is a long knife that the farmers use.]

"One girl is really fat; he calls her 'Grapefruit.' And when he gets punished and has to stand at his desk with his hands on his head, he sticks his tongue out at the teacher every time she turns her back. He calls her 'Godzilla.' I hate him."

Rosa leaves to go into the house; but before she enters she lets out a squeal. "Oh, my God!"

She has discovered Juan Carlos, sitting on top of the pile of oranges, throwing them off the porch. Hundreds of oranges are scattered in the dirt and in the bushes; and Juan Carlos, sitting high on what is left of the pile, has a big smirk on his face and an orange in each hand.

5

A SECOND ARRIVAL

ater that month I have a
chance to talk to Ramón's parents about military service.

Teresa, Ramón's mother, tells me, "It's going to be
very hard to see Ramón go off and do his military service.
When they first started the draft I thought, 'Oh, my God,
my son has to go too. What if they kill him?' And I couldn't
get used to the idea. I couldn't get it out of my mind. It
drove me crazy. All I could think was that I had to get
him out of the country somehow. But Marco says he should
do it, that in the army he'll learn to be a real man, with
responsibility.

"I try to think about it that way, but all I can think about is him there in the mountains, cold and hungry, and in constant danger of being killed. Sometimes I think, 'Why should my son die to defend the life of our president, Daniel Ortega?' Marco and I fight about it all the time. Marco says he has to go and defend his country, and I say, 'Oh, sure, so Daniel will live longer. Do you want your son to come back dead?'

"I know a case where these two brothers came back dead from the military service. Daniel Ortega sent them a wreath, and the mother just picked it up and threw it into the street. 'I don't want any flowers,' she said. 'I want my children back.' I told Marco I didn't want my children to go so that the same thing would happen to them. Just imagine, both her sons at the same time. At the funeral she picked up all the flowers and threw them into the air. She was totally out of her mind."

Marco has a different point of view.

"This war that is being waged against us," he tells me, "is stripping the dignity not only from the leaders but also from the entire population. It's the people who suffer the most. We fought a revolution to throw out the dictator. And we won. We were proud. There is nobody who knows how to love their country the way Nicaraguans do. And now there's this war. Ortega doesn't want this war any more than the people do. Who has the duty of defending the people's dignity if not the youth? Are they going to send the old men into the mountains?"

After two months with the Riveras, I leave Nicaragua for a little while; and when I return, I come in by plane. No border crossings or buses this time. It's all worked out. I have called Marco, given him my flight number, and asked him to pick me up at the airport.

My trip through customs is not very thorough; all

zippers are opened but nothing is removed for more careful inspection. The German couple in front of me, on the other hand, longtime residents of Nicaragua returning from a vacation, undergo an item-by-item search. The inspectors end up confiscating jars of oregano, parsley, and basil and send the couple on their way. Apparently customs officials are worried about marijuana smuggling, and the dried green herbs look very much like crushed marijuana leaves.

I walk outside the modern air terminal to wait for Marco. Fifteen minutes later, I am still waiting. A huge, luxurious airport bus, the only luxury bus I've ever seen in Nicaragua, swings around in front of me, empty. I smile at the driver, shaking my head in response to his silent question, and continue waiting. I figure I'll give Marco an hour.

Nicaraguan time is different from time in the United States; it's much more relaxed. *En punto*, "on the dot," never is. A two o'clock appointment often means that you'll meet at three or four or five. "Later" can mean days; "I'll stop by tomorrow" can sometimes mean weeks.

So I wait and look around. The season has changed. The air is cool, and there's a soft breeze. The airport is full of arriving foreigners; tomorrow is a government holiday celebrating the revolution, and dignitaries from around the world are coming to show their support for the Sandinistas. There are young people in their teens greeting the planes; they are speaking French and German and English and Russian as they check off names on the clipboards that they are carrying.

The airport bus comes by again. We nod and I wait some more. Another half hour goes by. The bus does two more swings. I continue to stand there, surrounded by my baggage, looking, I suppose, forlorn. Finally, I'm ready to give up. Just as I begin to look for a cab, the bus arrives a fifth time and stops in front of me. The door opens.

"Can we give you a ride?" asks the driver's assistant. The bus is still empty.

"Where are you going?" I ask.

"To the Intercontinental Hotel."

It's closer to where I'm going than the airport, so I climb on. And this giant bus takes off toward town with me as its only passenger.

"Are you coming here to work?" asks the driver.

It is a logical question. There are thousands of foreigners in Nicaragua, working to help the struggling country. Especially technicians and professionals. In the days of Somoza, only those people who had money could afford to go to college. When Somoza left, many of the wealthy and educated left, too, fearful of what the new government might do to people who had money. Doctors, engineers, scientists, agronomists, and many others left Nicaragua for other countries; and Nicaragua was left with a terrible shortage of trained people, and a desperate need for them. So there are a lot of foreigners from the United States, from Europe, from Australia, from Cuba, from Russia, who have come to help.

The bus driver is surprised by my answer.

"I'm writing a book," I tell him, "about young people in Nicaragua."

We are speeding down the road toward the Intercontinental Hotel.

"Oh," says the driver. "I have kids. Would you like to meet them?"

"Sure, why not?"

Five minutes later he turns off the highway and begins maneuvering his monster bus through the narrow streets. He turns down dirt roads and winds around shacklike houses on what appears to be more a footpath than a road. As we move we kick up swirls of dust in every direction. People stand in front of their homes staring at us. I feel as though I am on board a runaway bus in some TV cartoon. Then, finally, he stops and we get out.

I meet his kids and his wife and drink a fresca while sitting in a rocking chair on a dirt floor.

"Okay," he says half an hour later. "Now where can I take you?"

I tell him where I'm going. Ten minutes later, we pull up in front of Grandma's house in my private bus. The crowd from the porch, kids, adults, neighbors, and even two boys who are selling newspapers, swarms around us, as amazed as they are impressed by the giant, fancy bus that has delivered me.

The driver's assistant unloads my bags, and the driver steps out to say good-bye.

"What do I owe you?" I ask.

"Nothing," he says, shaking my hand and getting back into the bus. "Que le vaya bien." Have a good time. And he takes off.

I walk into the yard. Marco's car is sitting there with the hood up and half the parts on the ground. My friend Marco is stretched out in a hammock.

Sometime later, Ramón and I are sitting in rocking chairs on the porch. In the west the sky is filled with gray clouds that are streaked with the sunset: Slashes of orange and yellow and purple and pink pierce the gray. Juan Carlos is sitting on Angela who is screaming like the parrots' imitation of her. Rosa, who loves organizing things, is playing hopscotch with two neighbors and her sister; she has drawn the board in the dirt in front of the porch. And Grandma is sewing dresses for three of her grandchildren out of a set of sheets that her daughter in Canada has sent her. "They're much too pretty to sleep on," she tells me. Pretty printed fabrics are hard to find in Nicaragua.

The scene is not much different from the one I left

two months ago: kids playing, Grandma sewing, Juan Carlos tormenting Angela. But the *sound* has changed. In the time I was gone, Traca Traca arrived.

Traca Traca is a toy: two solid, heavy plastic balls about an inch in diameter at either end of a string about twelve inches long. There's a knot in the middle of the string. You hold the knot between your thumb and index finger. Then, with a rhythmic up-and-down movement of your hand, you get the balls to swing out and hit each other above your hand, below your hand, above your hand, below your hand, above your hand—traca, traca, traca, traca. The point of it is to keep them going as long as you can—traca, traca, traca, traca, traca, traca, traca, traca, traca, traca. The trick is rhythm and steadiness. It's hard. After days of borrowing Traca Tracas from the kids so I could try, I finally succeed in doing it ten times. I never get beyond ten.

The noise of the plastic balls hitting each other sounds like the keys of a noisy typewriter hitting the roller. And when it's done right, the balls hit each other rapidly and rhythmically, making the same sound as a good typist. The sharp snap of the sound travels for blocks.

Kids who have mastered Traca Traca can do it forever. And this November in Managua, it seems as though every kid in the city has mastered it. Traca Tracas are an obsession. All of Managua sounds like one huge secretarial school.

Against a background of Traca Tracas, Ramón and I sit talking about his involvement with the Red Cross.

"Right now," he says, "I go every Saturday. We learn lifesaving and first aid. If the war comes to Managua, it could, I think it probably will—the contras bombed the airport a couple of years ago you know—if it comes, it'll be really important for us to know first aid. When I was little there was a war here. People died right on this porch."

The porch we are sitting on, his grandmother had told me, was the neighborhood emergency hospital—the porch and the living room of the house. The battles took place just around the corner.

"When school vacation begins in December," Ramón tells me, "I'll be going to Red Cross practically every day. By the time vacation is over, I will have earned my first aid certification."

The December-January vacation in Nicaragua is the long one; it's the equivalent of the summer vacation in the United States. In Nicaragua, the kids go on to the next grade in February. One of the reasons for this schedule is that coffee is harvested in those months, and teenagers, even city kids, are needed to bring in the crop.

"I'd rather be in the Red Cross than the army," Ramón says. "The Red Cross doesn't fight. They're not even allowed to carry guns in their ambulances when they go into the battle zones. I'd rather work with them in the war zone than have to shoot."

"The Red Cross is supposed to be neutral," I say. "If you came across an injured contra, what would you do?"

"Treat him."

Another day I ask Ramón if he ever gets into trouble at school. I know he's a good student, but I ask anyway.

He smiles. "Once I got into big trouble. In my school we have to do cleanup duties, and one time when it was my turn, there was a workshop going on in another part of the building, so the teacher left me and a few girls in the room, cleaning. The girls started arguing with each other, and I said to them, 'Cut it out. I don't want to work with loonies.' So one of the girls says to one of the others,

'Go tell the teacher he doesn't want to work with us. See what she says.'

"I lost my cool and said, 'What do I care about that old bag? She's as old and cuckoo as a bat.' And I said a few more insulting things about the teacher. I certainly didn't know she was standing at the door. Anyway, all six of us got called into the principal's office, and I got told off for saying what I'd said, and I had to bring my father into school the next day.

"He was furious. Before we got to school he took off his belt and said, 'Watch it, because whether you like it or not, I'm going to hit you in front of all your friends.' I was worried, but I kept quiet. When we got there, he was too shy to do anything in front of the nuns.

" 'I'll give you a good hiding, but at home, not here,' he said. But he never did.

"I know he loves me," Ramón concludes. "He says he loves me even more than the others because I'm his first son. And I believe that he punishes me for my own good, like he says. But that doesn't stop me from getting mad. If I could change one thing in my life, I'd change the way my father treats me."

Later that night I am in my room reading when I hear a huge explosion, followed by two more. I run out to the porch. The family is assembled there, everyone together, everyone frightened. And the street is filled with people, speculating, thinking the worst and trying to dismiss it from their minds at the same time.

Marco points to the sky in the direction of the airport. Even in the dark sky you can see the massive black clouds from the explosion. We are all thinking the same thing. Managua has been bombed. This is the beginning of an invasion. The war has come to the capital.

We turn on the television, but there is no news. Someone brings a radio out to the porch and we listen in silence. There is nothing about the explosion.

Finally, about half an hour later, a long half hour, the television announces that a fireworks factory near the airport has blown up. The war has not arrived.

Nor is it the war that brings the explosions to Managua at midnight on December 7. It's the celebration of Purísima, a religious holiday honoring Mary, mother of Christ. All night sporadic firecrackers and rockets have been leading up to the big moment when hundreds of thousands of explosives go off at once. The sky bursts into color, and the noise is deafening.

Purísima arrived on November 28. For weeks before its arrival I had heard people complaining. This year there would be no Purísima—there was no money to buy the baskets of candy, the food, the toys for the kids. On the buses the conversation repeated itself day after day, with different speakers. No money, no food, no toys. The same thing was being said about Christmas. In the old days, the "God Child" brought gifts; this year, there would be none. The country was in crisis; there was a war to feed and there wasn't enough left over to take care of the people. Like the Grinch, the war was stealing Christmas.

So Purísima explodes onto the scene, subdued. But people do not give up tradition easily. There is excitement and spirit as they walk the streets, visiting the hundreds of altars that are set up outside homes, altars to the Virgin Mary, decorated with draped fabrics, Christmas lights, sparkles, flowers, branches, and always an image of the Virgin in the center.

Purísima lasts nine days, and people go from one altar to another singing hymns to the Virgin and collecting food and candy and gifts, simple gifts, like paper hats or toy brooms or masks. The gifts used to be better, I'm told.

On December 7 there is a government-sponsored Purísima celebration in a central square where professional altars have been erected and thousands of people go to sing and to stand in line for hours to receive a toy.

For many it is the only toy they will receive this season. Even for those who can afford to buy them, few toys are available. Nicaragua does not manufacture dolls that burp or cars that run on remote or robots that turn into spaceships. And there aren't enough dollars to import frivolous things like toys.

Marco and his family are going to have a quiet Christmas this year as well. His car died, or was about to, so he retired it. During Purísima, amid the constantly exploding firecrackers, Marco and a welder are working on a "new" car.

For three weeks now, they have been moving the parts from his old cab into a new frame. The old cab was falling apart; everything was rusted and corroded and in danger of collapsing; but the motor and the parts were still good. So Marco bought another old car, one that had a decent frame but a lousy motor. And, part by part, he put the old car into the new frame. Then he sold off the pieces of the old cab—windows, door handles, doors, bumpers, mirror, and so on.

One afternoon I am sitting in Marco's house watching cartoons on television: the Smurfs, the Flintstones, a cartoon from China, another from Czechoslovakia. In recent days I have seen *The Incredible Hulk*, Danny Kaye, and a face-the-people program that appears weekly in which President Ortega answers questions and listens to complaints from people all over the country.

Ramón is at the Red Cross. The younger kids are taking turns getting their baths in the outside sink. Teresa, Ramón's mother, is making a fire in an outside grill. They have a stove in the kitchen, but they don't have any gas. Tomorrow, Mario, the thirteen-year-old, will get up at five in the morning and go with the empty gas tank to stand in line. Last time he did that, he arrived home with the gas at four in the afternoon.

Great-grandma has fallen asleep in a rocking chair with a sleeping three-year-old in her lap. Gormío, the dog, is sitting in the yard, scratching. Just yesterday Gormío bit a neighbor who was playing in the yard. Marco punished him.

While I am watching a cartoon about Aladdin and his magic lamp, Marco, who has been working on the cars, comes into the house to get a tool. When he leaves, Gormío sits up and begins to growl. Marco lets out a howl and begins to run. I run out to see what's going on. Gormío takes off after him. Marco, who is overweight and a pretty slow runner, is moving as fast as he can. Just as they reach the mango tree, about fifty feet from the door, Gormío grabs on to Marco's shoe. Marco wiggles himself loose and climbs up the tree.

There is Gormío, looking up and growling. There is Marco, stuck in the tree. All I can do is laugh. My only regret is that Ramón is not there to see it.

I walk back to the porch and find Rosa reading a book to Juan Carlos. His eyes are red from crying, and I notice toothprints on his arm.

"What happened?" I ask.

"He grabbed Angela's stuffed animal and threw it off the porch. She bit him."

A day or two later I am planning a trip to a store for foreigners called the Diplomatic Store. Poor countries often have such stores in their capital cities to accommodate foreign diplomats or visitors. All those products that you can't buy in the markets are available for dollars in the "Dip Store." Most locals could not get their hands on dollars even if they could get in.

At the Dip Store you can find just about every kind of food, and clothes with designer labels, and electronics and blenders and towels and refrigerators. Stationery supplies. Cosmetics. Even a few car parts.

I hate going to the Dip Store. You walk in and feel as though you have entered a fantasy land, an exclusive one, that only you and a few other privileged souls can enter. The contrast between the inside of that air-conditioned store and the rest of the country is disturbing. You are reminded how unfair the world is. After my first visit, I vow never to go in again.

Why should *I* have access to all those things when people I have grown to love do not even dare to dream of them?

But I am about to break my vow. I have decided to buy the ingredients for Christmas dinner, the ones that are not available, so that Ramón's grandmother can make an old-fashioned, traditional meal. And maybe, I think, I will get a few gifts for the kids.

"What would you like for Christmas?" I ask Rosa before I go.

She thinks for a while; then she gets a big smile on her face. "A chocolate bar and an apple," she replies.

6

MAKING A REVOLUTION

It is *five-thirty on a Wednes-*day evening. Managua is always chaotic at that hour. The streets are filled with people coming home from work. Hundreds are hitching, spread out through fifty feet or so at either side of every bus stop—just far enough so that if a bus comes, they can run back and squeeze on. Occasionally a truck stops and people pile into the open back.

Other people are trying to catch cabs. But most of the cabs are already filled, every inch of space occupied. Still other people are standing in lines waiting for buses, lines that sometimes stretch forty or fifty feet.

I have been in line for twenty minutes, waiting for the 118; three 118s have passed without stopping; they were already packed beyond capacity. Each of them stopped about fifty yards past the bus stop to let out passengers; a few people ran and squeezed on.

I grumble to the woman who is in front of me in line, "Que barbaridad el transporte." How horrendous this transportation is! It's the usual opener for conversations on crowded buses or in interminable bus lines.

She is tall and thin; her black hair, permed, sticks out, making her face look tiny. Heavy blue eyeshadow and a light orange lipstick highlight her features.

We begin to talk. Maria is twenty-five; she works for the government. Ten minutes into a conversation about where I'm from and what I'm doing, I discover that Maria fought in the mountains during the revolution. Two Cokes and two hours later, I let her go home.

Maria tells me that she grew up in a family that had two maids, a cook, and a mansion. One morning in 1978, when she was fifteen, she packed some things in her book bag, said her usual off-to-school good-byes, and disappeared into the mountains.

"I couldn't stand living the way I was living," she says. "While my parents were partying with Somoza, while I was going to the best schools, while my friends and I were swimming at the club, there were thousands of campesinos [peasant farmers] starving. Babies were dying of malnutrition and diarrhea and diseases that could have been prevented. Even though I was young, I knew that Somoza didn't care that most campesinos never even saw a doctor in their whole lives. He only cared about getting richer.

"I first started thinking about poverty when I joined a church group. We used to talk about the cruelty of poverty and about the real meaning of religion and Christ's message. We talked about how we all had a responsibility to change things, to help the poor.

"That started me thinking about injustice. Through the church we organized some demonstrations, but nothing changed. The demonstrations would get broken up by the Guardia, and people would get hurt. In those days there was a lot of opposition to Somoza from practically the whole population. There were strikes and fasts and marches. But the more the opposition grew, the more the repression grew. It got so a lot of us got really frustrated and angry.

"Then one day the Guardia killed a good friend of mine. She had been marching peacefully when the Guardia threw tear gas into the crowd to break up the demonstration. People started running and screaming. There were shots; and she was dead. She didn't even believe in violence.

"That's when I decided that nothing was ever going to change until we took up arms. Somoza wasn't going to change, and he certainly wasn't going to turn over the power to anybody else. Elections were a farce because the Guardia counted the votes.

"I had a friend," Maria continues, "who was a student in the university. He told me one day that he was leaving school and going to fight with the FSLN in the mountains. He arranged it so that I could go with him."

"Did you tell your parents what you were doing?"

She laughs. "They would have locked me up."

The FSLN (Sandinista National Liberation Front) was a group dedicated to overthrowing Somoza and his Guardia and to creating a society in which there wouldn't be such inequality between the rich and the poor. The majority of Nicaraguans were poor and powerless. The FSLN wanted to give land to the landless and "power to the people," regardless of their wealth.

The people in the FSLN called themselves Sandinistas. Because they were young they were called *los muchachos*, the kids. And in 1978, when Maria joined, many of those young people were in the mountains, launching attacks on Guardia posts, stealing weapons, and trying to recruit campesinos to fight with them. They believed that change could only come through organizing the people—especially the poor—and fighting a revolution.

"It was cold and wet in the mountains," says Maria. "There were times I used to think that I'd never get dry or warm again. And we lived with fleas and mosquitoes, ticks and lice; and we went to the bathroom in the bushes. And we were tired, always tired. Tired, cold, hungry, wet. A lot of us had come from pretty privileged backgrounds. We had no idea what it was like to suffer.

"And I learned what it meant to be hungry because sometimes we went days with nothing to eat. Mostly we ate the fruit that was growing wild; and we learned to eat monkey meat.

"But one of the most important things we learned in the mountains was how to share. We were all in it together. We had to help each other; our lives depended on it.

"Part of our job in the mountains," Maria tells me, "was to tell the campesinos that they could do something about the way they were living. We told them that we were fighting to change the system—that when we won the revolution, we would give them their own land and a voice in the government.

"Some campesinos joined us; they served as guides

and they learned to use guns. But most were too frightened. People were getting killed."

I tell Maria that a week ago I met a campesina who gave me a poem she had written when a young guerrilla fighter she knew was killed. I still had the poem in my bag.

To a Guerrilla Woman

In the mountains of Estansuela
I heard the songbirds singing
Because they had met Tania,
The woman guerrilla.

Oh, woman, young and beautiful,
You joined the guerrillas without concern
Of losing your life.
And you met the assassins who hated you.
Oh, Tania, how beautiful you looked
With your olive green suit and your carved boots
And your red and black scarf
And your gun at your side.

Oh, Tania, I watched you go by with
your friends and I knew
That some day you would be the first to die.

Alicia Yoreno Guido

"It could have been me," says Maria as she hands me back the penciled poem. "We all lived knowing we could die."

Maria and Tania fought in the mountains with guns. In the cities, there were other FSLN members who performed different functions. They "raised" money by robbing the rich; Daniel Ortega, now the president of Nicaragua, was jailed when he was caught robbing a bank to get money for the FSLN.

The city group also bought and stole guns. And they rounded up food and supplies and sent them to their *compañeros*, companions, in the mountains. They also tried to recruit the city poor and the workers to their cause.

In the cities a lot of children helped the FSLN; they were used as messengers to deliver notes and packages—children who were small enough not to be suspected by the Guardia.

One woman tells the story of a mission she performed when she was thirteen years old. Her mother had been working with the FSLN, and they had given her a package to deliver. The package contained boots, food, and a rifle.

At the time the roads were patrolled by the reserve corps of the Guardia, who would stop cars and buses and search for weapons. The woman recalls her experience in detail:

"To get a boxful of boots and some food through to the mountain zone was no problem; the problem was getting the rifle through. It hadn't occurred to anybody to take it apart so it could go through in pieces. They delivered it to my mama wrapped in a lined linen bag. My mama called me and explained that there was a rifle there, that it had to be taken somewhere else, and that if she took it they would very probably find it. Then she asked me if I dared take it; I told her yes.

"This was a measure of my mama's desire to participate, for in spite of the risk I was going to run, it didn't make any difference to her. I went in a public conveyance. The assistant or driver of the vehicle—I don't exactly remember—took hold of what I was carrying and of course felt its weight. He asked me what I was carrying. At that moment I didn't think and I told him I was carrying some candles for a first communion.

"It was absurd to take a few candles wrapped up in a linen bag—and besides, the weight itself—so the driver realized that it couldn't be candles, because of the weight and the way the thing was wrapped, and then he said to me: 'Better put this thing under your seat and when the First Reserve Corps comes, be asleep.'

"I went all the way acting as if I were asleep, and when the bus stopped, everybody got off and I stayed there asleep. Then the driver told the guard who was going to make the inspection: 'Wait, I'm going to wake the girl; she's my responsibility.' But the guard said, 'No, let that young one sleep.' And they didn't make me get off and didn't lift up the seat. They were even looking underneath the bus and everything. That is how we got the rifle through.*"

Today, that little girl, Doris Tijerino, is the chief of police of Managua.

There were other, even smaller kids, involved as messengers. One boy used to carry messages from one "safe house" to another. A safe house was one where the people were in sympathy with the FSLN, but nobody but the FSLN knew it. When guerrillas from the mountains came down into the cities, they would stay and meet in safe houses. The boy, who was about ten at the time, also delivered packages from the city guerrillas to the guerrillas who were in the mountains near his house. He'd been doing it for months when the Guardia got suspicious,

* from *Doris Tijerino: Inside the Nicaraguan Revolution*, as told to Margaret Randall.

and he knew his life was in danger. So he put on a wig and a dress and girls' shoes; he put barrettes in his hair and a bracelet on his wrist; and, disguised as a girl, continued his missions.

Other young people went out at night with spray cans and painted the walls: "A free country or die," or "Long live the FSLN," or "Death to Somoza." The "wall campaign" was vitally important to the Sandinistas. They wanted to popularize their cause and to create the idea that there were lots of Sandinistas all over the place. The more walls that were painted, the more their presence was felt.

The Sandinistas didn't have any other way to promote their cause. They couldn't give speeches on street corners because they would have been jailed. They couldn't knock on doors and talk to people because they never knew who would turn them in. Everything had to be done in secret; there were *orejas* all over the place. (*Oreja* is the Spanish word for "ear." In this context it means "spy.")

And they certainly couldn't present their revolutionary talk on the radio or TV or even in the newspapers; the media was controlled by the government.

So they did it with graffiti—and kids.

One young man tells me, "When I was around twelve, I would tell my mother I was going to my friend's house to study or that we were going to a movie. A whole bunch of us would say the same thing. And then we would meet on the street and pick where we were going to do our painting. We needed a lot of us because we had to post people all up and down the street in both directions. It took maybe six of us to do the signs. We had signals, like a certain noise or a whistle or a bird sound that meant somebody had seen a Guardia or an unknown, and we'd better take off.

"Wherever we were, we knew which houses were safe. If we spotted the Guardia and we had to run, we knew which houses we could go into. We'd go into houses, through backyards, over fences, and into other houses. We didn't only paint; we glued posters on houses, especially houses where we knew Somoza sympathizers lived. And sometimes we worked with stencils too."

"You were young. Did you realize how dangerous it was when you were doing it?" I ask him.

"Oh, yeah. We knew we could have been killed. In those days you could be killed just for being on the street at the wrong time. Most of us had seen people being killed; if not in real life, we saw it on television. Sometimes they'd publicize it just as a warning for the rest of us."

"Did you do it for the cause or because it was exciting and dangerous?"

"We were making a revolution."

"Were you fighting to help the poor?"

"Most of us were fighting to get rid of Somoza. We were fighting for freedom. It was exciting, sure; but we understood that we were fighting to free Nicaragua from the dictator. And we also understood that every time we went out we were risking our lives."

Waging a revolution was indeed dangerous. No one dared speak openly of his or her involvement—not to the family, not to friends, not to teachers. The country was full of spies. Neighbors turned in neighbors; teachers turned in students; and relatives sometimes reported on the activities of their own families—sometimes for money, sometimes for favors, sometimes out of fear.

"I remember walking down the street one morning with my mother," a young lady from the town of Estelí tells me. She was thirteen at the time. "We saw a crowd of people and walked over to see why they were standing there. I'll never forget it. There was Doctor Ochoa, his wife, a girl who lived with them, and their dog, all of them bloody and dead, lying in the street near their house. Their necks were slashed. The doctor had been supplying the Sandinista guerrillas with medicines. He'd been careful, sending the packages with kids and having them drop them places so there was never contact between two people. Someone obviously turned him in."

The bodies in the street served as a warning to any would-be sympathizers.

The worst repression came when the FSLN began to gain in strength. In the beginning, in the sixties, the FSLN posed no threat to the government. Most of the early opponents of the dictatorship were idealists who talked about equality and sharing the wealth—young people mostly, who had neither the money nor the support to do much damage. The muchachos who took to the mountains in the sixties and early seventies didn't have much of a chance of overthrowing the government.

"We called them 'muchachos locos,' [crazy kids]" says one woman. "We knew they didn't have a chance against the Guardia. We all thought they were risking their lives for nothing."

But nature and greed helped them out. In 1972, when the earthquake shook Managua, a lot more than buildings cracked. The thin veneer of support that propped up the Somoza regime cracked as well. The active opposition now moved beyond the muchachos. After the earthquake, the entire country could see the abuses of power. Everybody watched as Somoza, his Guardia, and his friends grew richer while the people suffered—not just the poor, but the middle class as well.

Businessmen, who had always quietly supported Somoza because they had been able to flourish under his rule, were infuriated by the way Somoza and his friends grabbed up all the profits to be made from the disaster.

And they were appalled by the corruption. In addition to the Guardia's selling things that had been donated by concerned countries around the world, millions of donated dollars disappeared. So in the aftermath of the earthquake, middle-class opposition surged. People were angry.

During those same years, from 1972 onward, the support for the Sandinistas grew as well. In the late seventies, what had started on the college campuses found its way into the high schools, into neighborhoods, into houses all over Nicaragua. One woman, a twenty-six-year-old nurse, tells me about how she got involved.

Elena was sixteen, pixyish looking, with tiny features and a sparkle in her dark brown eyes. Her family was poor, so Elena was brought up in her uncle's home. Her uncle was an officer in the Guardia.

The same thing was happening all over. One friend of Somoza's told an American writer, "No one here can trust his own sons . . . or his daughters."

Elena went to a public high school where the Sandinistas had set up the High School Student Movement. Like most teenagers, Elena liked doing things in groups.

"Actually, I joined because some friends said, 'Hey, it's really great belonging to this group. You'll learn a lot. And besides, we've got to help get rid of Somoza.' That was 1977, two years before 'the triumph.' I didn't know what it was all about; it wasn't until after I joined that I started reading the pamphlets that the college group sent down to us. They were the ones who got us on track. They used to tell us that we had to rise up against Somoza, that he and his people were exploiting us and had been exploiting our parents and their parents and all our relatives for years. They told us that as young people, it was up to us. We had to put up signs and paint the walls and get ready to fight.

"So we used to have meetings after school and talk

about our plans and listen to talks from the college groups. I used to tell my parents that I was going to the movies with friends or that I was going to study. It wasn't true. There were meetings, and sometimes we put up posters. We even made bombs and hid them in this storage area in the ceiling of one of the classrooms. We wanted to be ready in case the Guardia came to get us.

"At first the teachers didn't know anything about what we were doing. But in 1978 some of the teachers joined us. They especially helped us with money so we could buy paper and paint and other stuff.

"Then one day the Guardia grabbed some of our members and some university students. We stayed out of classes and had a hunger strike and demanded that they let our friends go free. They didn't tell us that some of them were already dead.

"Anyway, one day during our strike, we were meeting in the center classroom, and the Guardia arrived. Whenever we met in there, we posted students outside. They saw the Guardia coming and told us; and we started to dismantle the ceiling storage space and take out our bombs. But the Guardia just threw tear gas bombs at us and nothing happened.

"Another time, the Guardia came again, but we didn't have any warning. As soon as we saw them, everyone just took off in all directions. Some got away, some didn't. I remember that I had a big bandage on my hand because a couple of days earlier I had played volleyball with a basketball and fractured my finger. When the Guardia saw the bandage they picked me out and said I was one of those damned kids who went around throwing bombs and that I needed a beating. They told me to get into their jeep. I told them that the only way they'd get me into that jeep would be to kill me. Then one of them grabbed me by the hair.

"Just then one of the Guardia recognized me. My

uncle, who had raised me, was in the Guardia and this guy had been to our house. 'Don't touch her,' he said. 'Her father's a major.' He never knew that it was really my uncle. Anyway, they let me go. Then this guy who knew my uncle turned to me and said, 'Nothing happened, right?' Then he added, 'And don't say a word to your father.'

"He needn't have worried. There was no way I was going to tell my uncle that I had joined the revolutionary movement. He would have killed me."

7

TOWARD A UNITED FRONT

While Elena and her friends were meeting and making bombs, while Maria and her compañeros were attacking Guardia posts, while the younger kids were painting fiery slogans on walls, many other Nicaraguans were hoping they could get rid of Somoza peacefully. Their goal was to remove Somoza, reorganize the Guardia, and elect a new government.

This group of anti-Somoza people was mostly from the upper classes. They were professionals and business-people, people who owned land, people who had privilege. But they were not all rich and educated. There were also middle-class and poor people who opposed Somoza but feared bringing more violence to their country.

Many of them were also afraid of what the Sandinistas wanted to do once Somoza was gone.

The Sandinistas were convinced that Somoza would not leave unless he was violently overthrown, that the revolution would have to be bloody. But they also felt that the problems in Nicaragua were larger than Somoza. For the Sandinistas, getting Somoza out was only the first part of the revolution. The next part would be even harder.

The biggest problem of all was the enormous imbalance of power and wealth. While the majority of the people in the country were desperately poor, and powerless to do anything about it, a small minority had most of the land, most of the money, and *all* the power.

The Sandinistas felt that in order to change this inequality, the government had to redistribute some of that land and some of that wealth. And also the power. Poor people, they felt, had a right to be involved in the decisions that affected their lives. Money should not determine who has the most power; nor should it give some people power over other people's lives. One of the FSLN's slogans was, and still is, "Power to the people."

Many people in Nicaragua were afraid of the Sandinista goals. They wondered how it would be possible to give so much to the majority without taking it away from the comfortable minority. And how, they wondered, could the government step in and take over the economy without taking away some essential freedoms.

Many of the ideas that the Sandinistas were proposing were similar to the ideas of the governments that existed in Cuba and the USSR. In those countries there was no private ownership of businesses; the government owned and controlled everything. People worried that the Sandinistas wanted to do the same thing in Nicaragua.

By the end of 1977, five years after the earthquake, this was the situation in Nicaragua:

The Sandinistas were fighting for equality and against Somoza. Most of the Sandinistas were in their teens and their twenties. And many were children of wealthy and middle-class families.

The other anti-Somoza people, greater in numbers, were hoping to get Somoza out peacefully.

A large group, probably the majority, wasn't bothered much one way or the other. They accepted what they had. It wasn't fun; it wasn't fair. But that was life.

Then two things happened to swell the opposition to Somoza and to bring many of the nonviolent groups into the Sandinista camp. The first had to do with a man named Pedro Joaquín Chamorro.

He was the editor of the most popular newspaper in Nicaragua—and he was against Somoza. He was also well-liked and popular among the middle and upper classes, a member of an old and respected Nicaraguan family. The nonviolent, non-Sandinista group thought of him as the man who might replace Somoza.

Then, one Tuesday morning in January 1978, while Chamorro was driving to work, his car was ambushed by three men who pumped around twenty bullets through his windshield and into his upper body. He died before reaching the hospital.

When word of the assassination got around, all of Managua exploded in rage. People agreed that, of course, Somoza's men had fired the guns. On the day of Chamorro's funeral, people roamed the streets burning buses and breaking into buildings—and everyone noticed that there were more red-and-black Sandinista banners than had ever been seen before.

Within two weeks businessmen had organized a nationwide strike, and everyone in the country knew that the Somoza regime was in serious trouble. Over the next months, there were spontaneous uprisings in villages around the country, and the Sandinistas knew that their support had dramatically increased.

The second event that added dramatically to the strength of the Sandinistas was like a scene out of a movie. It took place on August 22, 1978. Everyone in Nicaragua was tuned to the radio to hear it develop.

Somehow the Sandinistas had gotten hold of two Guardia troop trucks and twenty-five uniforms of the elite Guardia troops, from the combat boots to the black berets. At eleven o'clock on a Tuesday morning, the two trucks pulled up at the National Palace, where Somoza's hand-picked Congress was in session. One truck emptied out in the front of the building; the other went around to the back. Twenty-five Sandinistas masquerading as Guardia started to enter the building. The uniforms they were wearing were those of Somoza's personal bodyguards.

"What's going on?" one of the palace guards is said to have asked when the troops arrived. No one had told them to expect these guys.

The answer from the guerrilla leader, reportedly was, "The boss is coming. Keep quiet."

The guards let them through. Upstairs were two more armed guards. The Sandinistas tried to take their guns. One of them resisted and was shot.

Then the Sandinistas stormed into the hall where Congress was meeting. The Sandinista leader fired some bullets into the air and shouted, "Nobody move!"

Everybody dived under the tables.

Other Sandinistas emptied the offices and hallways

at gunpoint until everyone in the building (some 1,500 people) was inside the big room. There were relatives of Somoza, friends of Somoza, members of all the leading families in Nicaragua. Somoza couldn't afford to send in the troops. He was forced to negotiate with his enemy.

And while the Sandinistas were negotiating with Somoza, they were also on the phone with reporters. For forty-eight hours, it seemed, every person in Nicaragua had his or her ear to the radio. In one house a woman named Mrs. Tellez sat listening more carefully than most. The reporters were talking about the leaders of the Sandinista group. One of them was referred to as "Comandante Dos," Commander Two—a young woman. No names were used.

In *Sandino's Daughters*, Mrs. Tellez says that as she listened to the reports, she thought of her daughter, Dora Maria, who had left home to join the FSLN when she was still a teenager. Mother and daughter had had no contact since. It had been years. Mrs. Tellez had suspected that her daughter was dead, but as she listened to the news reports, she thought that maybe Comandante Dos was Dora Maria.

Everyone all over the country was obsessed with the news reports. The people were in the middle of a real-life adventure, and the bad guy was losing. Somoza had been brought to his knees by the muchachos.

About forty-eight hours after it began, the siege ended. Somoza was forced to pay the Sandinistas $500,000 and to give them six pages in the newspaper to say whatever they wanted. He also released fifty Sandinista political prisoners and guaranteed transportation out of the country to the released prisoners and to the Sandinistas who had taken over the palace.

The day the Sandinistas boarded the buses and rode victoriously to the airport (taking hostages with them), the streets were filled with crowds waving the red-and-black banner of the FSLN and screaming, "Down with Somoza!"

Mrs. Tellez was one of the people in the crowd. As the buses went past the corner where she was standing, she caught sight of Dora through the window. Her daughter was indeed Comandante Dos.

The Sandinistas flew out of Managua in glory. With that one act, the FSLN had won the hearts and the support of nearly everyone in Nicaragua.

But it would be another year before Somoza would go. Not until his cities and factories and even churches were bombed by his own Guardia, and thousands more were dead, would he finally leave.

The final shove came in June 1979. By then, even Somoza was talking not *if* but *when* and *how* he would get out and *who* would take over when he was gone. On the highest levels deals were being made. Which country would fly him out of Nicaragua? Who would escape with him? Where would he go?

Many of those negotiating with Somoza were particularly interested in coming up with a plan that would dilute the power of the Sandinistas. Many people in and out of Nicaragua were afraid of the Sandinista plans to divide up the land, the power, and the wealth.

But by 1979, most Nicaraguans understood that in order to get rid of Somoza once and for all, everyone had to work together—businessmen, professionals, small landowners, the middle class, the poor, and the Sandinistas.

In June, in cities all over Nicaragua, there were "insurrections," little wars in which local muchachos, sometimes working with the Sandinistas and sometimes working on their own, seized power in a town and kicked the Guardia out—in many cases for good.

And in Managua, the Sandinistas had decided to

take over six neighborhoods. With the help of the people who lived in those neighborhoods and with the locally organized groups that the Sandinistas had been building for years, they would seize control of the capital city.

The plan was to build barricades that would seal off each neighborhood from the Guardia. Then they would set up command posts with armed guerrillas to fight off the inevitable Guardia attacks. The neighborhood where I lived with Ramón's family was one of the six.

"First we built the barricades," Ramón's grandmother tells me one day. "We did it pretty quickly because practically everyone in the neighborhood worked together. It was the women and children, though, who did most of the work.

"We built the walls out of paving stones from the streets. They were these six-sided cement tiles, just like the ones that are out there now." She points to the street.

"Somoza owned the factory that made the stones, and he made a fortune paving the whole city after the earthquake. They were supposed to be earthquake-proof because they weren't cemented down; they were just fitted into each other like puzzle pieces. It was especially nice to be building barricades against Somoza's army out of Somoza's own paving stones.

"Anyway, once the first stone was pried out, the others came up easily. Little kids were able to pick up the loose stones and carry them to the place where we were building up the barricade, and we used every bit of help we could get. All the families were out there with all their kids just carting those stones."

Elena, the girl who had joined the high school organization in 1977, remembers that the high school students

had been told that the insurrection would begin on
June 11.

"But it started on Sunday, June 10. I remember because I came out of mass and there was chaos in the
streets. People were running all over the place, into schools
and churches and the Red Cross. They were looking for
a place to stay because, they said, the war had begun.

"I went home and ate breakfast, and then I said to
my mother, 'I'm going.'

"And she said to me, 'And where are you going? This
is war, not a party.'

"And I said, 'I'm going to school to play.'

"And she said, 'Don't tell me that. Don't go.'

"And I told her I was going. I collected some papers
that contained FSLN material, and I took them with me
because I knew that if the Guardia should find them in
the house, they would harm my family.

"Then I went to school and met some of the other
kids who were working with the organization. We had
an assignment to walk the streets telling people that if
their houses couldn't sustain a volley of bullets, they should
look for places of refuge.

"We all went to neighborhoods where we didn't live,
so we wouldn't be recognized. We wore stocking masks
and hats, and we slept at the houses where the Sandinistas had set up their posts.

"One day I went back to see my parents. They hol-
lered at me and told me I was crazy, that I was just a
child and I was going to get myself killed. My parents
were really suffering because my two older brothers had
joined the Sandinistas some months earlier and nobody
had heard from them since. They begged me to stay home.

"But I didn't pay attention. When it got dark, I dressed
in dark clothes and went back to the other neighborhood.
There was a curfew and no one was supposed to be in the
streets at night. We used to get away with it because the

streets were really dark. The government had turned off all the electricity in Managua a few days after the fighting began. The water too, except for a dribble.

"My next assignment was to check everybody who came and went. The streets were barricaded and we held the neighborhoods. We wanted to be sure no undercover Guardia got through, but we knew people had to leave during the day to try to find food. They had to get permission from us to leave, and we would register them so that when they came back we could check them off. One day an old woman returned with a sack of beans, and I found a dismantled rifle in her sack and a pile of ammunition.

"At night, only those of us who were working for the organizations could come and go. We had passwords that changed daily. They were actually slogans. Like I would say 'Patria libre' [A free country] and the answer was 'O morir' [or die]. If we had the right answer, we could pass into a different neighborhood.

"One time I was guarding a corner, and a nun came along and wanted to enter. I said the slogan but she didn't give the right answer. She told me instead that she was on her way to help a young girl who had just had a baby. I told her the slogan so she could pass through the other streets.

"When we weren't on assignment, we used to write with spray paint on the walls. Finally, we could do it freely; we wrote messages to our friends who had been kidnapped and we wrote revolutionary slogans.

"I wasn't around on July 19 for the victory celebrations. About ten days after the war began, I was manning one of the barricades. We had a twenty-two rifle, machetes, clubs, and firecrackers. We used to throw the firecrackers and hope the Guardia would think they were bullets.

"They, of course, had very sophisticated weapons.

"At four o'clock one afternoon, while I was on duty, a tank pulled into the street and began to shoot mortar shells in all directions. One of them hit the barricade and bathed me with shrapnel. I really didn't feel anything, but I knew I'd been hit; so I said to my friend, 'Take care of my gun, I'm going home.'

"I went home without my gun because my mother would have died if she'd known I'd been using a gun; and besides, I had two younger brothers and it wouldn't have been good to carry arms into the house.

"Even though I was injured, I walked three blocks to my house. But when I got there, I couldn't see any more. The gunpowder had temporarily blinded me.

"I said to my mother, 'I'm tired. I feel as though I have a fever.'

"She looked at me and fainted because I was covered in blood. My father carried me to a clinic. Unfortunately, I spent the rest of the month in a hospital, one that was in one of *our* neighborhoods. That's where I was when the country was celebrating the victory."

The explosion that sent bits of metal into Elena's body was only a tiny part of the chaos and shooting and bombing that mangled Managua that month. Ramón, who was only six at the time, remembers smelling smoke constantly. His grandmother can stand on her street corner and point to the houses that were bombed by Guardia planes. And everyone remembers no electricity, no water, and not enough food.

"We slept underneath the table, all of us together," says Ramón's grandmother. "We put mattresses on top of the table and on the floor and we huddled together, terrified. Our house was the biggest in the neighborhood, and the Sandinistas asked us if we would serve as an emergency hospital. The main command post was at the bridge just around the corner. I remember being so scared when I told them yes. Once I agreed to use my house as a hospital, I could never say that I wasn't a collaborator.

"I remember saying to Marco, 'Maybe we could put a great big red cross on the roof and the planes won't bomb us.'

"He laughed. 'That would be giving them a great target.'

"I used to live in terror of a knock at the door. The Sandinistas used to say, 'Patria libre' and we had to answer 'o morir.' But we all knew that if the Guardia returned and wanted to get in, they would say the same thing.

"So we got to be a hospital, but there were no doctors. I was the doctor. I would bandage and clean and treat wounds. One time they brought in a young man covered in shrapnel. There were all these tiny bits of metal all embedded in his body. I spent hours and hours taking them out. I wasn't a nurse, and I'd had no training, but I guess a mother just can do things like that."

Ramón doesn't remember many details, but what he does remember he remembers vividly.

"I remember that my father was always out there fighting and that our porch and house were filled with injured people. I was terrified that my father was going to come home in a stretcher like all those other people."

Marco remembers too. "Ramón was frightened all the time. Every time I left the house to go to the bridge, he would scream. The bridge was where the battalion was. He was little, but he understood. Sometimes I was afraid he would die from so much crying.

" 'Please, Dad, don't go!' he used to scream, and he would start to tremble. Then it would seem as if he were losing his breath.

"So I would go for a little while and come back and go again and come back. When we went to sleep at night, I used to hold his hand; that was the only way he would sleep. If I wasn't there, he would scream, 'I want my daddy's hand!' 'No, that's not my daddy's hand!' he would shout when anybody else would try to calm him down.

"Toward the end of the month, the Guardia bombed the bridge, and Ramón and I went over to see the damage. There was blood and bodies blown up and corpses. Ramón, yes, he knew what death was, and suffering. He'd seen my mother treating wounded people, and he'd seen the pain on their faces. And he thought, 'My dad could get to be one of those dead people.' "

I find it interesting and understandable, when I hear this story, that Ramón has chosen to join the Red Cross and that he doesn't want to be a soldier and participate in killing. But I find even more interesting his answer to one of my questions.

"What do you dream about at night?" I ask him one day.

"Last night," he tells me, "I dreamed about some enemy planes. In my dream there was a searchlight that spotted them in the night sky. My friends and I were about to cross a bridge, and the bridge was on the verge of collapsing. Most of the people had already crossed and now it was our turn.

"Four of us step onto the bridge and it collapses. I manage to hold on to the edge, but one of my friends falls down, and all of us run to see if we can pull him out. The bridge was over a deep hole, like a huge canyon. We climb down and then climb back up carrying him. Then we climb a mountain and see another enemy plane which crashes into the sea. There's a huge crowd, and we see a car parked nearby. When we get close, we see inside the car my dad, my mom, and all my brothers and sisters.

"Then, in my dream, I get up for a glass of water, and there's this earthquake. When I go outside I see that everything has been destroyed. There is nothing and nobody around, just me in a huge clearing without houses or buildings, nothing whatsoever. So I walk around and begin to moan."

Even now, Ramón's dreams are about the revolution. On July 17, 1979, while the neighborhoods were still barricaded and the final bombs had not yet dropped, Somoza, his half-brother, various members of Congress, and around two dozen top Guardia officers—about one hundred in all—boarded two planes in Managua and got off in Miami, Florida. Somoza stepped into his limousine and was driven to his home on Biscayne Bay.

8

THE LITERACY CRUSADE

On the eighteenth, nineteenth, and twentieth of July 1979, they poured into Managua from the hills—the muchachos who had thrown out the dictator. And the people poured into the streets to dance with them, to drink with them, to dream their dreams together. There was ecstasy. There was enthusiasm. There was a dignity that these Nicaraguans had never known. And there was pride. The world was looking at this tiny country, and this tiny country was looking back with a patriotic fervor that surged inside every Nicaraguan.

The people would work together to solve their country's problems. They would tackle poverty and inequality and economic development. Nicaragua would become a model for all the struggling countries of the world. Finally, all Nicaraguans would work together toward a common goal.

Valerie Miller, an American author, was in Nicaragua when the spirit was at its peak. She writes:

"I remember the two young children of a friend, eleven and fourteen, working one Sunday after mass on a new public housing project for the poor. They, along with other neighbors both young and old, had responded to a government call for volunteers to help at odd jobs around the community on the weekends. The brother and sister, their clothes and faces streaked with dirt, were hauling bricks in a rickety wheelbarrow for a volunteer construction crew. They made a game out of it, laughing as they piled the bricks higher and higher. Stacking and carting, loading and unloading, they were a tireless twosome, despite the many bumps and bruises on their hands and arms incurred during their labors. When a priest friend came by and asked them what they were doing—if, maybe, they were helping to build a house—the young girl looked up at him, grinning widely, and said, 'No, Father, we're working on building a country. Do you want to help?' "*

The new government, set up before Somoza left by a coalition group consisting of Sandinistas, businessmen, religious leaders, and interested foreign governments, began immediately to enact reforms. There were housing projects and health projects and land projects. But the biggest project of all was the literacy crusade. The new government had inherited a country in which nearly half of the people couldn't read. Most of those people were

* from *Between Struggle and Hope*, by Valerie Miller.

campesinos, peasant farmers, who lived in places where there were no roads, no electricity, no schools.

Within days after taking over, the government was making plans to teach the campesinos to read. Thousands of people were needed to do the teaching, people who could leave their homes and families for five months, people who were strong and healthy and enthusiastic. People who were flexible, who could adapt to a different way of life, who would see the experience as an adventure as well as an opportunity. There was only one answer.

Kids. Students. From twelve years old and up. They would be the teachers. The government would train them, prepare them, and send them out into back country where they would teach the campesinos how to read.

The kids were up for it. Five months away from their homes. Five months away from their parents. Five months on their own, on a mission. They would serve their new government and show the world what they could do.

But the parents were scared. They knew it was dangerous out there. There were horrible sanitary conditions, polluted water, wild animals, perhaps even wild campesinos. Few of the parents had ever been to the places their children were going.

The government went on a campaign to recruit the young teachers. There were ads in the newspapers, on television, on the radio. There were billboards and posters. And speeches in schools and churches. A new army was being formed, an army without guns, an army armed with books.

Schools were closed and workshops were set up to teach the kids to teach. All over Nicaragua young people were telling their parents, "Everybody's going. You can't make me stay home."

There were family fights at the dinner tables. Boys and girls lied to attend the workshops, saying they were going to the movies, to ball games, to visit friends.

And they trained—physically with exercises, mentally with how-to-teach-reading workshops, emotionally with games and drama and cultural preparation.

And finally, on April 23 and 24, 1980, just nine months after the victory, 90,000 teenagers were ready to teach Nicaragua to read. Some 30,000 taught in the cities; 60,000 got on buses and left for the unknown.

Evenor Ortega was one of those kids. I interview him seven years later when he is twenty-three and a sublieutenant in the Sandinista army. This is an official interview, my first and only, set up by a friend, an army officer, who works in the press relations department of the army. I am ushered into a room and someone brings in coffee and a pitcher of fresca. My friend sits opposite me with a notebook on her lap. All official army interviews must have an observer.

Evenor enters a few minutes later. He is handsome in his uniform with its silver bars on the shoulders. Handsome, but a little stiff when he first sits down. After five minutes of reminiscing about his experiences in the literacy campaign, there are tears in his eyes.

"When I got to the plaza around six in the morning, I discovered that people had been there all night long, singing songs and lighting campfires and just being with their friends because the next day they were leaving each other.

"All our parents were crying and giving us advice because we were very young kids. They were saying, 'Look, don't do this, don't do that, obey the people you stay with, take good care of yourselves.' People were saying things like we would have to sleep next to snakes, and we should put garlic in our pockets to protect ourselves, and lots of other things like that.

"So the going away was very emotional, both happy

and sad. We were detaching ourselves from our homes for five months. We were leaving our friends, the life in the city, and all the conveniences that we had here in Managua. And we were going into the unknown.

"I didn't know what to expect from the campesinos. I thought maybe they would attack us or that they might boycott us. I was afraid because I didn't know how I would be received.

"There were around twenty buses; and when we took off, we were waving and shouting and singing—and scared. After a while, my bus became very quiet. People were crying and thinking about what was to come. But then we started telling jokes and singing and calling out slogans; and we were very, very happy. As young people we felt the experience would show that we were good revolutionaries with a real love for our country, and that as young people, we would prove how responsible we could be.

"So we left Managua at seven in the morning and arrived in Jinotega around four in the afternoon. We toured the town and ate in people's houses, and we all slept that night in a school building. We sang some more and made campfires and said good-bye again because we were all splitting up and going in different directions. We gave our best friends little mementos and things to remember each other by.

"A lot of the kids called their homes to say that they were fine and that we were in Jinotega and that it was terrific. Others sent telegrams. We had a great time there.

"The next morning we got up at four and it was incredibly cold. We got on trucks and we all went in different directions. My group was going the farthest, to San Jose de Bocay. En route, the truck I was in kept dropping people off along the way, so it took a long time. By four in the afternoon, we finally got to the end of the road; but we still weren't at the villages.

"We got off the truck with our books, our backpacks, our bundles. We were all wearing our uniforms—gray shirts, blue pants, and different-color backpacks. I was carrying the red-and-black Sandinista flag of my squadron. It was there that we each learned where we were ultimately going. I had expected that a group of us were going to live in one house and we'd go off to teach reading during the day and then come back and be together every night, laughing, playing, and enjoying ourselves. But I discovered that we were all going to be with different families, and our houses were very far from each other.

"The leader of the village where a bunch of us were going came to meet us with five mules to help carry our packs. There were thirty of us and the packs weighed a lot.

"I was carrying two backpacks because I had so much stuff. They had told us that there wouldn't be *anything* where we were going and that we had to bring whatever we needed. I was carrying clothes; books; a hammock; boots; a hat; underwear; foods like sugar, powdered drinks, rice, dried soup, and other instant foods; cookies; medicines; Vaporub, Merthiolate, alcohol, medicine for diarrhea, for headaches—for everything. I never knew anything about medicines until they gave me all that stuff. That day I learned it all. I had every kind of medicine. It was incredible!

"When I was packing, my parents kept adding things too. They would say, 'Take this,' 'Take that,' 'Put this in,' 'Put that in.' I couldn't get it all in one pack, so I was carrying two, one on my back and one on my front. When they piled the things on the animals, they discovered that everything didn't fit. I was left with my two packs. One of my friends helped me.

"That trip was my first experience carrying my things and walking in the mountains. I was exhausted. Really exhausted! We had done exercises in the city getting ready for this trip, and we had done a lot of walking, but in the city we used to rest every ten blocks and have something to eat.

"At midnight we arrived in the village where we stayed that night. The house I slept in was falling apart, and all the animals were inside with us—chickens and pigs. It was a horrible first impression. They gave us a supper of an ear of corn and black coffee. In Managua I was used to eating a real meal for supper: rice, beans, bread, cheese. It was a shock for us all. One ear of corn!

"The next morning we met all the campesinos in the village, and we were introduced one by one. The head of the village told everyone that we had come to teach reading; and then we were handed over to our families. Some of the campesinos had arrived with mules, but my family was too poor to have one, so I carried my backpacks.

"Before we left, the head of my group gave me a blackboard, chalk, notebooks, and pencils and said, 'Okay, you know what your mission is. We'll come visit you down the line.'

" 'No problem,' I told him, and I left with the campesino and his son. It was around eight in the morning when we left. We walked and walked and walked. We climbed hill after hill after hill. I kept asking, 'Is it nearby?' And he kept answering, 'Yes, very close.' 'Are we almost there?' 'Yes,' he would say; and we kept walking.

"After a while, they took my backpacks and I walked carrying nothing. I was still so tired. We just kept walking and walking and walking. Finally, just over a little hill, we came to the house, a poor little house with a straw roof, an earth cooking oven, a dirt floor. It was very small. I was so tired that I went right to sleep. When I woke up, I was very disoriented. It was all so strange. I didn't know how I was ever going to adapt.

"My 'father' introduced me to his wife and his seven children, all of them small. I was the only big one. That night we talked a lot. I told them who I was and where I was from, and I talked about the books and the literacy crusade. They told me about themselves and what they did, and where the river was that they bathed in.

"I gave all my food to the señora so she could cook it for everybody. Maybe it lasted a week. I gave her some uncooked noodles and I told her to make them, but she didn't know how. So she fried them up, hard, without cooking them first, just in oil. And her husband said, 'What is this?' And I explained that she had to make them with milk and butter; so she took them out and made them again, this time they turned into a big mush, like soup. That's how we ate them.

"I told them all about life in Managua. I told them about the people and how they dressed. These campesinos were very poor. They'd never seen a suit. And I told them about the buses and what the ocean was, and what a television was, and about trucks and cars and the movies. They had never seen many of the things I talked about, so I showed them pictures in magazines. I told them, 'This is a vehicle.' 'This is a movie.' I talked about everything that existed in Managua. Much of it they had never even heard of.

"I also told them all about my family, and after that we got along well. They loved me a lot.

"When I had gotten to know them, I took out the books and asked who was going to learn to read. I taught two families, both parents and children. I taught the kids in the morning and the adults in the afternoon.

"They had never had a school there. Most of them had never held a pencil. It was hard for them. They were used to holding a machete, which is a large object; their fingers felt stiff and awkward holding a pencil. They kept tearing the paper.

"Teaching for me was a real challenge. There was one man who used to say, 'I can't learn. I'm a very old man.' And I would tell him, 'You can do it,' and I would work with him until late in the night with the light of a lantern.

"The first thing I taught the campesinos was how to write their names. I would write a name on paper and explain that it was their name. And when they understood that those marks on the paper spelled their name they would take the paper and proudly show it to their family. Sometimes I had to explain over and over again that those marks had a meaning. And when I asked them to make the letters, they kept saying they couldn't do it.

"And when they finally learned to write the letters of their names, they wrote them everywhere: on boards, on the walls, in the dirt. They were so excited. And as they learned, they developed more and more confidence, and they discovered how great it felt to be learning.

"I had one kid who was very smart. He was twelve years old and I used to help him a lot, even when he was sitting and relaxing. He learned how to write his name and how to read the vowels and syllables. He was the first one to learn everything. After a while I decided that he already knew how to read. But he kept saying he didn't.

" 'Emilio,' I would say. 'Tell me what this says.'

"And he would say he didn't know. And I'd say, 'Come on, you know.' And he kept saying he didn't.

"Then one day his father gave me a 'cow contract'; and I said to Emilio, 'Your father gave me this contract for you to read.'

" 'I can't,' he told me.

" 'Read it,' I said.

"And he grabbed the contract and he started to read. He couldn't believe he was reading. He was so excited and so proud that he could do it; and especially he was proud that he could help his father in business. Finally he understood what it meant to be able to read.

"He ran around telling everyone that he could read, everyone he saw. He wanted to read everything. He would go to the store in town and read, 'Hay café,' there is coffee; 'Hay azucar,' there is sugar; 'Hay arroz,' there is rice. He read every sign and every label. Everything he was buying and everything he was selling. Everything that was written down. And he couldn't stop telling people, 'I know how to read!'

"The family was excited. Their oldest son had learned to read. And his excitement was the most beautiful thing! I couldn't even begin to recreate it. I felt so fulfilled, so satisfied. And when everybody else saw him, they wanted to learn too. I taught his father and the other kids and the neighbors. Everybody learned how to read.

"After I had been there for a while, my mother wanted to visit to see where I was living and what I was doing. So my campesino family and I got some mules and we went to pick her up. When she saw me she was astounded. There I was with my machete.

"She brought books and dishes and clothes and medicines. And she explained to the señora how to cook noodles. But when my mother saw how I was living, she was upset. She looked at the house and said it was going to collapse, and she cried and told me I should go home with her.

"It's true. It wasn't an easy life. It rained a lot, and it was muddy, and there was lots of wind. But I felt terrific. For me, everything was good. I felt so fulfilled.

"I learned a lot from the campesinos too. In Managua I lived with my parents and four brothers and sisters. I guess you could say I was more or less spoiled. I never worked in my house. But in the country I did everything because part of our mission was to work in the fields. I learned so much. Wow, did I learn!

"I learned how to plant corn and beans and how to harvest them. I learned how to pick coffee beans and how to milk cows. And I learned how to eat foods that were very different from the foods I ate in Managua.

"But the first thing you learn out there is how to carry a stick and a machete when you're out walking. One day I was almost bitten by a poisonous snake. I stepped on a branch and the snake was crawling up my feet. The twelve-year-old was behind me. When I jumped, he killed the snake with his machete. If I hadn't jumped, he would have slashed my foot with the machete. That day was horrible. I was so shaken I couldn't eat. That snake was huge. It was a yellow-bearded snake, and it could have killed me or affected my brain and left me crazy. The nearest doctor was four hours away.

"The longer I lived there, the more I learned to adapt to their ways. At first they had to take care of me and tell me what to do. But after a while, I didn't need any help. It was really a beautiful change for me. It was marvelous.

"When the crusade was over, we were all sad. My campesino family was crying. They made a great going away dinner with chicken and *nacatamales* [a sort of stuffed dumpling wrapped in a banana leaf] and corn on the cob. They gave me a chicken and a pig and corn to take home. And cookies for my mother.

"The father told me that if I wanted I could come back and live with them. That they would give me a piece of land. He said I could bring my girlfriend.

" 'This cow,' he told me, 'is yours whenever you want to come back.' "

Evenor is tearful as he finishes his story. When he returned to Managua, he brought the father and son with him to show them city life. And he brought his souvenirs, his gifts, his new skills. But for him, as for the many other young people I spoke to, the greatest gift of the crusade was the pride they felt for having achieved their goals, the newfound confidence they had in their own capacities to change the world, and the success of their mission (406,000 students passed the literacy exam).

"There was so much more to do for the poor people of Nicaragua. The crusade taught us how to give. We knew that what was coming would not be easy, but we had made a pact with the revolution," says Evenor.

And they kept their pact, those kids. Seven years later, while I am interviewing young people in Nicaragua, I discover that the most committed, the most idealistic, the most revolutionary Nicaraguans are those who participated in the literacy crusade.

"I had changed," says Evenor. "I was more independent, more mature, more responsible. I had become someone who could sacrifice for the revolution. I had become a man."

9

PROBLEMS

For Evenor, and for most of the *brigadistas* who participated in the literacy crusade, the experience of living with the campesinos changed forever the way they would view the world. For the first time in their lives they saw and understood what poverty was.

One woman told her young reading teacher, "Somoza never taught us to read—it really was ungrateful of him, wasn't it? He knew that if he taught the campesinos to read we would claim our rights. Ay! But back then, people couldn't even breathe."*

* from *Between Struggle and Hope*, by Valerie Miller.

"Back then," most campesinos assumed that their children and grandchildren and great-grandchildren would live pretty much the same lives the family had always lived—farming the land of the big landowners, serving them in their homes, deferring to them in life. One campesino from a tiny, tangerine-producing village, who is now working on a government-owned farm, tells me: "The man who used to own this land left the country with Somoza. I belonged to him for forty-four years—lived on his land, worked every day from five in the morning until eight or nine at night. Never had a vacation. Never had a doctor. My kids never had an education. I knew that I would work for him until I died and that my children would too. Didn't have a choice. There was nowhere else I could work."

Campesino dreams were limited. They didn't include education. Thumbprints were good enough for signing documents. And the Campesinos trusted their bosses to pay them honest wages; there was no need to know math. Many campesinos believed that they were incapable of learning how to read.

The revolution changed all that. Suddenly the campesinos were being told that education was their right. "I'm a sixty-year-old grandfather," said one man, "and have nine grandchildren—five boys and four little girls. I want them to know that everyone can learn—even me. You see, when I was young, I didn't have a chance to get an education. Now if they see me studying and see that me, an old man, can learn, well maybe they'll study harder. Then, they can do better and go farther with their lives than me."*

The young people of Nicaragua had brought dreams not only to the campesinos but also to the country as a whole. When the literacy crusade was over, one of the

---

* from *Between Struggle and Hope*, by Valerie Miller.

teaching supervisors, a priest, wrote: "The crusade has been carried out by the kids of Nicaragua . . . intelligent kids, sacrificing, determined—idealists and realists all at the same time. For me, the principal lesson of the campaign is that now Nicaragua knows that it can count on this treasure for its future. Not all the best children died in the war. With the living, we can carry out the other necessary wars to be fought, the war against social injustice, the war against poor health, the war against disease. . . . Thanks to their efforts, Nicaragua will be totally different in the future. It will be a better nation, a nation that all Nicaraguans deserve."*

And in the beginning, it was. In the first two years after they took over, the Sandinistas not only ran the most successful literacy campaign ever, they also sent health brigades into the mountains. Just as the literacy crusade had taught thousands of young people to teach reading, the health campaign taught thousands how to vaccinate and administer medication that would prevent polio and measles and tetanus and typhoid and all the other diseases that the advantaged people no longer got.

And the health brigades also taught mothers what to do when a baby had diarrhea, because campesino babies still died of diarrhea. And they taught the campesinos about the dangers of poor sanitation so that diarrhea and other diseases that were related to poor sanitation could be prevented.

And the Sandinistas also began an agrarian reform program in which the government helped the campesinos set up cooperative farms where they were their own bosses and made their own decisions. The government gave the campesinos land that had belonged to the big landowners who had left Nicaragua. Somoza himself had owned nearly

* from *Between Struggle and Hope*, by Valerie Miller.

a third of the farmland in the country. And there were plans to divide up other lands that were lying idle.

And the government took over the banks and gave out loans to help the cooperatives get started. In the Somoza days, small-time farmers couldn't get loans from the banks. Now, they not only got loans but the government also sent out advisers to help the campesinos solve agricultural or financial problems.

In those early years, many Nicaraguans were filled with pride and hope. They had thrown out the dictator; they were solving the problems of the campesinos; they were working together—the people and the government—to make life better for the majority of Nicaraguans.

So they all should have lived happily ever after. Except they didn't.

From the moment the Sandinistas took over the government, there were people both in and out of Nicaragua who wanted to get them out.

There were the Somocistas. They were friends and relatives of Somoza and former government and business leaders who had profited from and participated in the abuses of the Somoza years. They were afraid that the Sandinistas would take revenge because, historically, as soon as revolutionaries win, they usually put the old leadership in front of a firing squad or they chop off their heads. The Sandinistas surprised the world by outlawing the death penalty; but nevertheless, most of the Somocistas took their considerable wealth and left the country. From outside Nicaragua, many of the Somocistas were trying to figure out how they could get their country back.

There were the anti-Somoza businesspeople. They had participated in the fight to get rid of Somoza. They had cooperated with the Sandinistas; but many of them had never agreed with the Sandinistas' ideas of giving "power to the people" or of equalizing the gap between the rich and the poor.

The businesspeople knew that in order to enact the Sandinista plans, the government would have to control the way business was conducted. Many in the business and professional community were reluctant to give that much power to the government.

It was also clear to the business community that, in order to run a government for the welfare and to the benefit of the poor majority, power and property would have to be taken from the privileged minority.

Many in this group stayed and tried to participate in the government. Some of them were given important positions through which they hoped to influence the direction the new government would take. But it became clear in the first year of the revolutionary government that the Sandinistas had the upper hand—and that "power to the people" meant "power to the people who agree with the goals of our revolution."

Some of these early collaborators of the Sandinistas in the fight to overthrow Somoza resigned their government positions in the first year; others became disillusioned in the following years. A few left the country, disappointed, angry, and feeling betrayed—and became political leaders of the contras.

There was also the old Guardia. Some of them were tried and either freed or sent to jail. But many fled the country, especially the officers. They were in Guatemala and Costa Rica and Miami and Honduras. And *they* were angry too. They had been humiliated by a bunch of muchachos.

The old officers were organizing and talking to each other about how they would take control again. But they needed backing. They did not have enough money of their own to wage a war against the Sandinistas. In time many of these old Guardia officers would become the military leaders of the contras.

The ordinary soldiers of the old Guardia were also opposed to the new government. Some began attacking Sandinista literacy workers in the mountains of Nicaragua. They stoned houses where there were literacy classes; they raped brigadistas; they killed seven workers and threatened to kill any campesinos who participated in the lessons.

In the beginning, just after the Sandinista victory, these ex-Guardia soldiers operated alone or in barely organized and badly trained small groups, with little money for equipment and little hope of success. But by 1981 they had begun to organize a guerrilla army, popularly known as the *contras*, for *contrarevolucionarios*—people who are against the revolution. And eventually, they became one of the best-equipped, best-trained, best-funded guerrilla armies ever. The organization, the equipment, the training, and the money—most of it—came, and continue to come, from the United States.

Of all the groups who were opposed to the Sandinistas, the United States was, and still is, the most powerful. When Ronald Reagan ran for president in 1980, the year of the literacy crusade, one of his promises to the American people was that he would work to overthrow the Sandinista government. And he has kept that promise.

While the brigadistas were teaching the campesinos to read, and the health workers were vaccinating against polio and measles, Reagan was telling the American people and the world that the Sandinistas were terrorists.

While the contras were killing doctors and teachers and blowing up buses full of civilians, Reagan was calling the contras "freedom fighters" and sending them grenades, advisers, and more guns.

During the years of the Reagan administration, the

United States used its power in the international community to get other countries to help the contras and to
prevent Nicaragua from getting loans from international
money organizations. In 1985 and again in 1986, the United
States refused to trade with Nicaragua. That meant no
parts for American products—Marco's car, his mother's
sewing machine, the pumps that bring water to the people
of Managua. It meant that Ramón could not buy the tape
player he dreams of owning or the Nike sneakers he sees
on the tourists.

In 1987, on the same day that the newspaper, *Nuevo
Diario*, showed coffins of children being carried to the
cemetery, victims of contra bombs, Reagan asked Congress in Washington to give him more money for the
contras so he could continue his fight to bring "democracy
and freedom to the Nicaraguan people."

And, later that year, the people of the United States
discovered that even after Congress had passed a law
prohibiting the government from aiding the contras, the
Reagan administration was—illegally—pouring millions
of dollars into the contra military campaign.

"Why is Reagan doing this to us?" fourteen-year-old Karla
asks me.

Karla, like thousands of other young people in Nicaragua, is an active member of Sandinista Youth, an
organization that supports the goals of the revolution.
Karla speaks English; she has an uncle who is a doctor
in the United States, and she has spent several summers
with him.

"Nicaragua is poor," she says. "We are underdeveloped. How can we possibly be a threat to the United
States?"

There are tears in her eyes as she talks about the
plaque in her school that memorializes the boys who have

died in the war and about her friend Ricardo, who will be in a wheelchair for the rest of his life.

"Why is Reagan doing this to us?" she repeats at the end of our conversation. "He must be crazy!"

I have asked the same question: Why *is* the United States trying to overthrow the Sandinistas?

I have asked it of academics; I have asked it of U.S. government people; I have asked it of friends and relatives who agree with Reagan. Some have answered me for hours, others for minutes. But essentially the answer is always the same: Underlying the U.S. policy is the fear of communism.

The Reagan administration believes that the Sandinistas are communists and that there is an international communist conspiracy to take over the world. Those who support the contras believe that if the Sandinistas are permitted to survive, they—and their communist friends—will be a threat to freedom in the United States.

The Sandinistas claim that they are not communists; that while some of their ideas for solving the problems in Nicaragua are ideas they share with communism, other parts of their program are different. They say that their revolution is not modeled after any other revolution but tailored to Nicaraguan needs.

The United States is afraid that the Sandinistas will permit communist Russia to set up military bases on Nicaraguan soil. The Sandinistas have said that they are willing to sign a document promising not to allow a foreign military presence in their country and that they would allow international inspections to see that they are keeping their word. The U.S. government says it doesn't believe the Sandinistas that communists can't be trusted.

Another question I have asked is, Does the United States have the right to interfere in the internal affairs of Nicaragua?

The answer I have been given is that since 1823 the United States has assumed that it has the right to "protect" its own interests in Latin America, both business and political. Many times before now the United States has worked to overthrow governments that it does not like, governments that do not agree with the United States. It has even passed laws giving itself permission to send marines into other countries to "protect" U.S. interests.

The U.S. marines virtually controlled Nicaragua from 1912 until 1933. The marines finally left after the United States had recruited and trained a new Nicaraguan national army—the National Guard (the Guardia)—and handpicked the commander of that army—also called Anastasio Somoza, the first of the Somoza rulers. Within three years Somoza, with the help of his army, was president.

While Somoza and his sons were in power, the United States had nothing to worry about. The Somozas did whatever the United States wanted them to do. And when the first Somoza turned out to be a corrupt dictator, the United States continued to support him because he was an anticommunist. In fact, President Franklin Roosevelt was quoted in *Time* magazine as having referred to Somoza like this: "He may be a sonofabitch; but he's *ours*."*

The United States is the most powerful country in the Western world, and in Central America it has nearly always gotten its way.

* *Time*, November 15, 1948, p. 43

A young nursing mother carrying a gun has become the symbol of the women's movement.

The Rivera family percussion band

Nursery school class on the move

*Sandinista soldiers in
San Juan de Rio Coco*

*Mother of three young men
killed by the contras*

Hanging out

Teenagers take a break from harvesting coffee

*Making a pyramid at
a holiday celebration*

The dove of peace

10

FAMILIES IN THE WAR ZONE

fter two months of talking to people in the cities of Nicaragua, I decide to visit a campesino village that three months earlier had been the scene of a contra attack. The village, Quibuto, is in an area of Nicaragua that is considered a war zone.

A visitor or a journalist can travel almost anywhere in Nicaragua and talk to anyone freely. There are no restrictions except for war zones. In order to travel to these dangerous areas where there's been recent contra activity, you need permission from the army.

—

Marco is driving me to the army office in his cab. We were supposed to have left at 8 o'clock. He arrives to pick me up at 10:30. I grumble and instead of talking to him, I sit and read *Barricada*, the FSLN newspaper named for the barricades that were built from paving stones.

A front-page story describes an explosion in one of the border towns. A group of women and children were riding in the back of a pickup when the truck hit a contra mine. Ten dead, four of them children.

"I feel so ashamed of my country and what it is doing to the Nicaraguan people," I say, unable to continue my silence.

"It isn't your fault," says Marco. "Every Nicaraguan understands that it isn't the American people who are doing this to us. It's the government; it's the Reagan administration."

Everyone says the same thing—government officials, the papers, people on the street: "It isn't your fault. We love the American people. We know that it's Reagan, not you."

The first time I heard that idea was when I was in line for the bus on my first day in the country. A campesina, sitting on a big white bag filled with beans, had said, "It isn't the American people. The people are our friends. It's the government who is our enemy."

At first I didn't understand. How could they separate the people from the government? If another country were killing *my* kids and burning down *my* schools, I'd be filled with anger at the people of that country as well as at the government.

But eventually I realized that the Nicaraguan people had lived with a government under Somoza that did whatever it wanted to do. It followed that they would believe that a government's policies have nothing to do with what the people want.

Now I understood how the Nicaraguans could separate the people of the United States from the government. But I was not sure that I agreed with them. The people in the United States (unlike those in Somoza's Nicaragua), vote in free elections, and if they disagree with the president, they can vote for someone else. Since the people of the United States had reelected Reagan in 1984, they either agreed with what he was doing, they didn't know, or they didn't care.

I did care. I had come to Nicaragua to see if I could find out for myself what was going on. Reagan had said over and over again that the Sandinistas were terrorists. But so far, after three months in the cities of Nicaragua, I have seen no indications of terrorism on the part of the Sandinistas. Now I am eager to visit the war zone and talk to people who are directly affected by the fighting.

Marco pulls up at the army office and waits while I present my press credentials and ask for permission. Two more trips and two days later I finally have a letter of permission. I walk out of the press office, rent a car and am soon on the road, with a photographer, to a town around two hundred miles from Managua and an hour's drive from Quibuto, the war-zone village that had been attacked by contras.

At eight the next morning, we are outside our hotel giving the car its requisite push-start. Push-starting cars, and even trucks, is almost a tradition in Nicaragua. If you're driving alone, there is always someone walking down the street who offers to help.

Before we drive to Quibuto, we have to present our letter of permission to the local army office. And we need another letter from the local officials who monitor more closely the safety of going into a war zone. We had tried to get the local permission the day before, but had been told to come back in the morning. Things could change overnight.

The kind of war the contras are waging is not the kind in which soldiers take fixed positions and shoot at each other. It is a war of surprise attacks, of ambushes, of blowing up storage tanks, or of burying explosive mines on the roads—mines that are triggered when a car or bus or truck rolls over them.

The mines are usually planted at night; in the daylight hours they become just some of thousands of bumps in a dirt road. I have been warned that driving down those roads in a war zone requires intense concentration on the bumps. One friend of mine, who drives the roads daily with a companion, says they joke when they see a boulder in the middle of the road. "Which way do you think they want us to swerve, to the right or to the left?" they ask each other, laughing in their fear.

It is 8:05 when we arrive at the army post, and we are told that we cannot leave until after 10:00. The assumption is that by then, if there are mines on the road, they will have been triggered by military vehicles or by cars and trucks carrying Nicaraguans. They do not want foreign journalists getting blown up.

It is nearly 11:00 when we reach the turnoff to Quibuto. The road is blocked by four soldiers with guns slung over their shoulders. They wave us on after they inspect our letter.

The photographer looks off into the tree-filled hills. "This kind of terrain is the perfect cover. There's no way you can tell if there are contras in those trees or behind those hills."

We concentrate on the dirt road. It's the rainy season, and there are ruts and holes and rocks and tire tracks. There's not a chance we'd recognize a mine by a bump in the roadbed, so we settle for trying to maneuver our low-slung car without scraping its bottom.

One eight-inch-deep river and thousands of bumps later, we see the village. As we get closer, we notice a jumble of men, women, dogs, chickens, and kids about twenty yards from the road in an open space between two houses. We pull over to see what's going on.

We get out of the car and walk down the hill toward the crowd. There is a bright red mass of color in the center of the activity. When we get closer, we realize that the red mass is a slaughtered steer that is being cut up for meat. The animal has been skinned, and the skin is spread out on the ground like a bloody leather blanket. The trunk of the steer, still warm, is resting on the skin. Off to one side is a giant, white misshapen ball, three times the size of a basketball. I ask what it is.

"The stomach," says a man. "It will be cleaned and the lining will be used to make rope." He shows me a braided rope made from stomach lining.

Only the head looks as if it was once alive. It is still attached to the carcass, but it hasn't been skinned. The eyes are staring out at the crowd.

Two men are cutting off hunks of meat and sending them up to the porch of a house where they are being sold. Every eight days, says a campesino who is standing next to me, they butcher two steers for the 2,000 residents. In Managua buying meat means standing in line with your plastic bowl, sometimes from five until ten in the morning. In Quibuto, it means hanging around, gossiping, flirting, talking while the steers get chopped up.

The dogs—there are fifteen of them hanging around—love the activity too. They keep sneaking up whenever they can to steal a hunk or at least a lick. There are a couple of kids with sticks assigned to keep the dogs away.

The dogs are hard to look at. In this village, like

most poor villages where food is scarce, the dogs are skinny. Really skinny. Their ribs stick out because there is no flesh between the skin and the bones. At the base of their backs, the bones are practically poking through their skin.

"Are you here for long?" asks a man after first asking where I am from.

"A few days," I say.

"I live over there," he points. "Come and have a coffee."

"What do you think of Nicaragua?" asks a woman.

"It's beautiful," I say. "But most of all I like the Nicaraguan people—their friendliness, their openness, their courage."

"We just want to live our lives in peace," she says. "Where will you stay?"

There is no hotel in the village.

"I am looking for Benito," I tell her. Benito is the leader of the community, and we had been told to ask for him. "Can you tell me where he lives?"

"He's in town. He won't be back until this afternoon. He lives por allá," she points.

Por allá, "over there." A popular phrase—in the cities and in the villages as well. It's the answer to, "Where?" "Where can I buy bread?" "Where is there a hotel?" "Where does Benito live?" *Por allá*, usually accompanied by a hand gesture in some vague direction, is considered an adequate answer. No specifics necessary. The assumption is, I guess, that you will probably not understand complex directions anyhow and are better off walking in the right direction and asking again later.

"That's okay," I say. "We'll just wander around."

"I live por allá." She points in a different direction, silently inviting me to visit.

A few minutes later I am standing on a cement wall outside the school. In front of me are two burned squares of earth, the remains of two of the houses that the contras destroyed in their attack. I peer through the chain link fencing that serves as windows of the school; there is no glass. Inside the classroom are simple wooden desks and a big green blackboard along one wall. Another wall is punctured with bullet holes.

I walk toward a long line of identical houses, simple houses with dirt floors and wooden walls and roofs made of corrugated metal. In front of the houses, about thirty yards away, is a precipice that looks out over a valley and off into distant mountains. There is a woman standing at the edge, looking up at the soft white clouds that are speckling the blue sky. She is wearing a pink skirt and a white blouse, and with the lush green mountains as a backdrop, she reminds me of Julie Andrews in *The Sound of Music*.

I walk past the houses, which seem relatively new, and stand near the woman.

"Buenos días," she says, smiling.

We begin to talk. She is eighteen, pretty, with long dark hair falling over her shoulders and down her back. Ana and her family have been in Quibuto for three years. They were moved here by the Sandinistas, along with the other families in her village, a village close to the Honduran border that had been subject to numerous contra attacks and visits.

"The contras used to come into our village and go after the people who worked for the Sandinistas—the teachers, the health workers, the leaders of the CDS [the Sandinista 'people's' organization]. They'd kill or torture or kidnap them. And they'd run around saying how they were doing it in the name of God and how the Sandinistas wanted to abolish religion. Whenever the contras came, they would try to get the men in our village to fight with them. That's how they'd get their army. They'd say that the Sandinistas were going to kill our children and burn down our houses. And that they were fighting to stop them.

"And if the men wouldn't go voluntarily, the contras would kidnap them and hold knives to their throats and make them say bad things against the Sandinistas: how the Sandinistas were communists and would kill everybody who believed in God.

"The contras used to tell the men they kidnapped that they, the contras, would kill their whole families if they didn't join the fight against the Sandinistas. I know it because a lot of the men and boys would escape and come home and tell us.

"But I also know a lot of boys who are fighting with the contras voluntarily. At least I think they are. They left and never came back. They're either fighting with the contras or they're dead."

"Do you support the Sandinistas?"

"They took us away from our homes. They made us come here. There were a lot of people in our village who wanted to stay even if it was dangerous. Especially the old people. They just wanted to be on their land and in their homes. The Sandinistas forced all of us to move, even if we didn't want to."

Ana invites me into her house and introduces me to her brother. He is twenty-two and expects to be called into the Sandinista army any day. He doesn't want to go. He too knows people who are fighting with the contras.

"I don't want to shoot my cousins," he tells me.

"Did they go voluntarily to fight with the contras?" I ask.

He smiles. "The last time anybody saw them, they had guns in their backs."

I say good-bye to Ana and her brother and wander

some more. Quibuto and other new settlement villages all over the country are the Sandinistas' answer to attacks and forced recruitment by contras in border villages. It is widely known that the contras get their soldiers from these villages, both willing soldiers and kidnapped ones. The Sandinista strategy is to get the people out, both for their own protection and to cripple the contras' recruitment efforts.

It is a strategy that is creating a lot of negative feelings toward the Sandinistas. There are a lot of campesinos who would rather live with the threat of death than leave. They want to farm their own land, smell the dirt and the trees and the fields that they have lived with all their lives. From some parts of the country there have been reports of Sandinistas using violence against campesinos who refuse to leave.

There is something ironic about moving whole villages away from their land so the people can come to new villages that are also under attack. Ana and her brother experienced that irony. Quibuto's attack came on May 3, 1986.

It was almost five o'clock in the morning. Many of the women and teenage girls were already up, milling corn for tortillas, grinding coffee, getting the fires started in the stoves.

Men were getting ready to go to the fields to work on the coffee plants. Roosters were calling back and forth to each other from nearly every yard.

A few militia soldiers were on guard duty, but most of the militia, the local men who protect the village but are not part of the official army, had gone to a party the night before in a nearby town and were unable to get transportation back until the morning. The contras are believed to have known that.

At 5:00 A.M., the contras stormed in, shooting, shouting, throwing grenades. Some people ran out of their houses and into the underground shelters they had dug. Others huddled in their houses, peering out through the cracks.

One woman reports that the contras entered her house. "They accused me of harboring a piri ['rabid dog,' the contra slang for a Sandinista] and I answered no. I just had my two children with me. They grabbed my nineteen-year-old son and took him from the house.

"I followed them, pleading and crying and begging them not to take him. I said that he was my only hope in life, that I needed him to help me with the harvest. They said, 'No, we're only taking him for a little walk. We'll be back soon.' But I went back to the house crying because I knew I'd never see him again."

"What did they look like, the contras?"

"They looked like us," said another woman. "Poor campesinos who probably had families somewhere. They were wearing green uniforms just like the Sandinistas, except they had yellow hats and the fancy waterproof backpacks that they get from the United States."

In the five hours that the contras were in charge of Quibuto, they killed one man, who apparently gave them a hard time; they destroyed fourteen houses and five public buildings, including the health center and a meeting hall. They shot up the school and blew up a brand-new truck that the community had just bought. They destroyed a food storage warehouse that had just been stocked with food and supplies; and they raided and machine-gunned the walls of a building that had been inaugurated only a few days earlier, the children's dining hall.

The dining hall for children had been the project of a group of people from Spain. It was to provide milk and a balanced meal once a day for the children in the village.

The contras entered the new hall, dumped the milk that was there, destroyed the food, and then tried to set the place on fire. The wood was green, and the fire was struggling to take hold when an eight-year-old boy sneaked in after the contras left. As legend tells it, the little boy "peed out" the fire and saved the dining hall.

For five hours the contras controlled the little village, throwing grenades, screaming, shooting off their guns, and searching for certain target people. They were especially interested in finding the teachers.

To the contras, teachers and schools represent the good things that the Sandinistas are doing for the campesinos. The contras know that through teachers and schools, the government brings positive change to the campesinos. And the contras know too that it is in the schools that the children learn about the revolution and the Sandinista ideas.

Since the goal of the contras and the United States government is to turn the Nicaraguan people against the Sandinistas, burning down schools and kidnapping or killing teachers are special goals of the contra offense. Positive change does not serve the contra plan.

Estela is a teacher in Quibuto. I meet her the morning I arrive in the village; she and her seven-year-old daughter, Geysel, catch up with me as I am leaving Ana and walking toward the burned-up truck.

When Estela discovers that we are planning to stay for several days, she invites us to stay in her house. "I'll have to be sure it's all right with my husband first," she says. It is.

We unload our things into the simple house made of sticks and mud and corrugated metal sheets. The floor is dirt and, like the other homes in the village, there are no glass windows, only a wooden hinged square that swings in and out. Nor is there electricity. A 1984 contra attack blew up the power source for the whole village.

On the morning of the contra attack, Estela and her family were inside their house. They heard the shooting from the guns and the explosions from the hand grenades; they smelled the smoke from the burning buildings. And they heard the contras screaming for Estela. Somehow the contras had found out she was a teacher and were trying to find her house.

While the family held each other in terror, the contras entered other houses asking for Estela and the other teachers. They never found Estela, but among the eight villagers who were eventually kidnapped, one was a teacher and two were children, a fifteen-year-old boy and his twelve-year-old sister. All but the teacher eventually escaped. The teacher has never returned.

"We were all frightened," says Estela, "but it's the small children who are most affected by this war. My little girl still suffers from nerves. Whenever she hears gunshots, she stops eating and runs into the other room. She starts pacing the floor, her legs begin to shake, and she grows paler and paler. 'Oh, Mommy,' she cries, 'the contras are going to come and they'll take you away.' I see the same frightened behavior in the other children in my class."

I ask Estela about the kidnapped children. They are her husband's cousins. I ask her if she thinks I can talk to them; but Estela explains that the boy is in school in Managua and the girl doesn't talk to anyone these days— has barely talked at all since she came back from her capture by the contras. Instead, Estela brings me to meet their mother.

"It was the worst moment of my life," the mother tells me. "I now know that it's better to eat tortillas and beans with your children than to be rich and eat anything you desire without them.

"The contras came into my house because I'm the

closest to the road. They asked me for milk and I gave them some. They were surprised that I had it because I'm so poor, but someone had given it to me as a present. I gave it to them because I was frightened. Even though they're people like us, they're armed, and I kept thinking about all the horrible things they do.

"I tried to talk to the contras, but when they were ready to leave, they said to the children, 'Let's go.' It's what they said to everyone they kidnapped. 'Let's go.'

"I begged them to leave my children in peace. I told them that my husband was killed in 1975, and that I was very poor, and that I needed my son to help me. They never said yes or no. They just took the children and never came back.

As the woman talks, a hen and six chicks walk across the floor between us. In the other room, her sister is making tortillas with a rhythmic slapping noise. We talk for an hour, and the slapping noise accompanies our entire conversation.

"The contras took the kids with them into the mountains. Those kids were always cold and hungry. The only thing they had to eat was the fruit from the trees, some oranges, and some green bananas. And that was only once in a while. The rest of the time they were hungry. They had to walk and run and climb in the mud, in the rain, in the heat. But the worst was that the kids had to be with them, hiding, when the contras were attacking other villages. They saw shooting and killing. It was only by a miracle that they came out alive.

"It was during one of the battles that my girl escaped, sixteen days after they took her. The day she got free, everybody was resting. She was sitting near a tree trunk when there was an attack by the Sandinista army. The contras all ran away, but my girl was too exhausted. She couldn't walk or run any more, so she hid for an hour or so in this big hole in the tree trunk, waiting for everyone to go. Then she traced her steps back the way she had come.

"She remembered that they had passed a house not too far away. She started walking about two o'clock in the afternoon, and she found the house at about five. She just stood in front of that house and started crying. A woman came out and my girl begged the woman to take her in. She stayed there three days.

"The woman waited until someone she trusted came by. These days you can't trust anyone. You can't tell the difference between the contras and the Sandinistas. You never know if it's a contra dressed up like a Sandinista or a Sandinista dressed up like a contra.

"Finally, a man she knew came along. He took my little girl to the Sandinistas. When they told me, I didn't believe it. But when I saw her, I was like a hen who had found one of her lost chicks. I was out of my mind with happiness. My boy escaped later on Mother's Day. It was the best present I ever had. I can't stop thanking God for saving their lives.

"Of course, it wasn't over when they got home. My daughter was different. She was quiet and hardly ever spoke, even with her friends. She just sat there looking sad, and she slept a lot. And she couldn't stop eating. She was so thin when she got back. She just kept eating all day, beans and rice and cheese.

"Sometimes I look at my children and I think, 'Oh, how I love them and how we have all suffered.' Other times I look at them, and I feel all full of energy and happiness to know that I'm with them and that I can carry on fighting next to them.

"Sometimes I wonder. Here are these two armies fighting and we campesinos are caught in the middle.

"I beg God to give us peace so that we can bring up

our children. I can't understand why the contras burn houses. They say it's because they're the houses of militia men and Sandinista soldiers. But is that our fault? We mothers don't like the idea of our children being in the military service; but the law says they have to go. What can we mothers do? My son is fifteen, the one who was kidnapped. Soon he'll have to do his service. He needs to study, but instead he'll have to fight. I am a humble and ignorant campesina. I don't understand why we have to fight."

There are tears in our eyes as we hug good-bye. I don't understand either.

The photographer and I bump into Benito, the village leader, as we are walking toward his house. He is a tall, handsome man and he welcomes us to Quibuto and asks if we have a place to sleep for the night. Then he invites us to have dinner at his house. We rush back to tell Estela that we will not be eating with her. She seems disappointed. There is so little food, yet she is eager to share it with us. We promise that we will eat with her tomorrow.

As we approach Benito's house an hour later, there are three boys—three, five, and seven years old—wrestling on the porch. At first they are laughing and punching and rolling. Shirtless, shoeless, a fling of arms and legs. Then the mass takes shape and the two older boys make a toy out of the smallest, bouncing his shoulders back and forth between them. And then they pick him up. The oldest boy holds him under the arms, the other takes his legs, and they swing him back and forth, laughing.

"He's Reagan," calls the seven-year-old. "Let's throw him out." And they dump the little one off the porch.

"Hi," says a girl in a pink blouse, green skirt, sandals, and a big smile. "Sit down." We sit on a wooden bench.

Celina is twelve years old, tiny and pretty. She has big brown eyes and hair down to the middle of her back, tied with a ponytail elastic, the kind with plastic balls that intertwine. She tells us that her mother is in town until tomorrow, buying bread that she will bring back to sell. Benito is not there either. Celina is in charge of our dinner. She brings us a fruit drink in orange plastic cups and returns to the stove where she is cooking over firewood.

The boys come inside and we exchange names. They giggle shyly but stay.

While Celina cooks, the boys entertain us with songs. As the rice and beans sizzle, the sun goes down and soon we are sitting in the dark, watching the fire play games with Celina's tiny frame.

Before long Celina lights a small metal lantern and puts it on the table. Now the boys play shadow games, first with their bodies, then with their hands and arms and fingers. Finally Celina hands us plastic plates, each with beans, rice, boiled bananas, and two pieces of meat, surely the meat that we had met in the morning.

When Celina joins us, I ask if I can tape-record some of their songs. The kids are thrilled. Celina too. For the next half hour they sing—school songs, church songs, radio songs—at the tops of their voices. Celina directs the show, deciding what to sing and when to stop. There are shrieks and laughter when I play back the tape. For those minutes Celina is a twelve-year-old girl anywhere in the world.

We say good night, thank Celina for the dinner, and find our way back to Estela's house. The night is black, and the sky is bursting with stars. There is a magnificent silence, a serenity, a peacefulness that can only exist in a place where there are no lights, no cars, no motors.

Early the next morning I see Celina again. She has already cooked breakfast for her father and brothers. Now she is at the place where the women wash clothes. Like the other women, she is scooping water out of a barrel and scrubbing the clothes on a big stone. Each woman is washing on her own stone. There are girls as young as seven helping their mothers with the family laundry. Celina waves.

Later in the day Celina and I have a chance to talk. I ask her if she thinks about the contras.

"All the time," she tells me. "I'm worried that they'll come again and that I'll be in charge of the boys and they'll find us and kidnap us. Last time I grabbed the kids, and we ran into the shelter. We didn't have time to take clothes, and we were cold and scared.

"And I worry that they'll get my father. They were looking for him, you know. They were calling his name because he's a leader, and they know he's with the Sandinistas. Maybe they'll get him next time."

I ask her what she would do if they came again.

"Some of my friends say that they would shoot the contras if they came again. I'm too much of a coward to handle a gun. If I had to fight I don't think I would be very brave. I don't like to carry a gun and shoot. I know how, but I don't want to. Some girls say they would, but it frightens me. I'd try to hide. Last time I ran into the underground shelter with the boys, and we just stayed in the shelter, listening to the shooting and the shouting. I was scared and I still am."

"Why do you think the contras are doing this?"

"I don't know. I think the United States wants our

land and our resources. It's the United States that gives the contras their weapons. But I really don't understand why they want to kidnap children."

The next day Benito introduces us to two men in the militia who take us for a tour of Quibuto. The men are wearing uniforms and carrying submachine guns over their shoulders and hand grenades in their belts. As we walk people stop to talk to us and to invite us into their homes. They tell us how happy they are that we are there to see what it's like in Nicaragua because they know we'll go back and tell our people that the Nicaraguans want peace.

It's almost a refrain. I hear it wherever I go. "We want peace." "We don't want any more of our children to die." "Go home and tell your people. . . ." And the one that always brings tears to my eyes, "Our children are dying; the mothers are crying."

I wonder. Would Reagan continue this war if he were here with me, talking to these people? Would the men and women in Congress be considering funds for the contras if they could see the Nicaragua I am seeing?

We stop to talk to a thirteen-year-old boy who is in the militia. He is sitting in a hammock in the middle of the room, wearing his olive green uniform.

"Why did you join?"

"To protect my country against the Yankee aggression."

"What do you know about the government of Nicaragua?"

"I know that it is the government of the people."

"Why do you think the United States is giving money to the contras?"

"To make war on us."

"But why?"
"I don't know."

One of the men who is giving us the tour tells us that he fought with the contras.

"One day while I was working in the fields, the contras came and captured me and a bunch of others. We walked in the mountains for four days without eating or drinking anything. We were all simple campesinos. Like most of the other contras we met, we didn't know anything about politics. We believed the lies that they told us about the Sandinistas. And we also believed them when they told us that if we didn't fight, they'd kill us. So we fought.

"Months later I escaped. If they ever come again, they won't take me alive. We all have to fight so the Nicaraguan people can be free."

11

THE ARMY

iggling to the reggae music that is blasting from the PA system, posing and cavorting for the photographers, flirting with the female journalists, petting the parrots, the deer, the dogs (mascots who have shared their battles), these Sandinista soldiers are probably the most ecstatic, euphoric, insanely happy bunch of people I've ever seen in my life. They have lived for two years on the constant edge of death, never certain that they would be alive the next day. And now they know. They have survived. Wiser, more responsible, and more committed to the revolution after two years of "political education," they are going home. Just one ceremony, a few speeches, and a four-hour ride to go.

The ceremony reminds me of a high school football rally with cheerleaders leading the gang in home-team chants: "Aquí, allá, el Yanqui morirá." Here, there, the Yankee will die. Except the "Yankee" is not a sports team, it's the United States; and the game is war.

The speech, by the head of the army's Department of Political Direction, is reminiscent of the many other speeches I have heard in the last months. There are a lot of speeches in Nicaragua—by the president, the vice president, the heads of the various departments, other government officials. After a while all the speeches begin to sound alike. Even the most committed Sandinistas often go about their lives while their leaders call for vigilance from the TV screen into an empty room. There are only so many ways to say the same thing. I sometimes think that maybe, in the hallway outside the top government offices, there is a big barrel, filled with sentences and key words. Anyone who has to make a speech pulls out a few key words and an abundance of sentences; then he or she assembles them on a separate piece of paper and puts the originals back.

The key words for today's speech are *dignity, peace, courage, defense,* when referring to Nicaragua; *Rambo, intervention, shameless, invasion,* when referring to the United States. Key sentences: "We will never accept the kind of democracy [that they have in the United States] that means millions of unemployed, rampant discrimination, drugs, and prostitution," and, "we will not lick anybody's boots," "there is no price for dignity," and, "we will continue our fight to normalize relations with the United States, but in the event of an invasion, every worthy Nicaraguan will represent an annihilated marine. . . ."

There are a lot of fidgeting soldiers during the speech.

They've heard it before too. Mostly they just want to get onto those trucks and buses and head for home.

Then, finally, they're released, battalion by battalion; and they take off, cheering, leaping, laughing, running for the buses. Free to go home, in a caravan, to the thousands of Nicaraguans who will greet them with flowers and food and soda and beer and cheers as they enter Managua. To little brothers who will beg to carry their backpacks; to mothers who will hug their little boys with tears and relief, "little boys" who have become men.

But while the soldiers are running toward the buses, a subdued group of mothers and honored guests watches them. As they observe the ecstasy, they fight back tears. They are the families of soldiers who didn't make it.

Among the most knowledgeable, committed, revolutionary Nicaraguans are the ones who have learned in the army about the revolution and its goals. Once, two long years ago, these soldiers were kids, most of them in their teens, playing their radios, hanging out, going to parties, combing their hair. Most of them had learned about the revolution and the war in school; but school was school and the important things in life happened outside the classroom. Most of the soldiers who were leaping and cheering and shouting revolutionary slogans at the ceremony had entered the army reluctantly, some more reluctant than others.

Take the boys from the campesino village of Flores (not its real name), for example. Flores is a five-mile walk from the nearest town down a dirt road. There used to be a pickup that ran back and forth a couple of times a day, carrying people; but the owner of the pickup left his wife and moved away with his truck, stranding not only his family but also the whole village.

It's a quiet village that smells of flowers and clean air; its fields are bursting with beans and corn, and the path to the river is awash in the reds and oranges, yellows and purples of wild blossoms. Monkeys skitter in the treetops as you near the river, about a thirty-minute walk from the center of the village.

The campesinos in the village weren't much bothered by the Guardia in the old days; and today, there's no contra activity anywhere nearby. Flores is far from the borders; and when you're there it's easy to forget there's a war going on. Maybe that's why there's not much enthusiasm on the part of the Flores boys to join the army.

Ever since the pickup took off, cars and trucks hardly ever come into Flores—and never in the middle of the night. So when the army jeep comes to collar draft dodgers at one in the morning, the whole village wakes up; and the over-seventeen-year-old boys take off through the woods for the river.

"Why do you run?" I ask one of the boys.

"I don't want to die," he says. "I just want to be left alone to go to school and to help my father in the fields."

If there were no war, if there were no contras, if there were no ambushes or bombs or mines, there probably wouldn't be a draft. But there is a war. And there is a draft. Seventeen-year-old boys have to register, and when they're called, they have to serve. It's the law.

During my stay in Nicaragua, I talk to a lot of young men who are draft age. In answer to my question, "How do you feel about military service?" the usual answer is, "Hay que cumplir." One must fulfill one's obligation.

But there are many young men, like those in Flores, who hold out as long as they can. They don't register, and they try to avoid the recruiters as long as they can get away with it—that is, until they're caught. In the cities, they "get caught" at parties, at parks, at the movies, at discos, or at baseball games like the boys in Bluefields one morning.

Bluefields is a city on the east coast, on the Atlantic Ocean. Somoza and his Guardia didn't bother the east coast much; there wasn't even a road from Managua to Bluefields until recently. The people there, many of them, don't identify with the people in Managua.

For close to two hundred years the British occupied the east coast; and more than half the population of Bluefields is black and English-speaking, descended from West Indians who settled there in the early 1900s. There is a significant population of Indians as well, who speak Indian languages. Many of the people on the Atlantic coast are members of the Moravian church, which does not support the revolution.

In many ways the east coast is like another country.

When the Sandinistas announced a compulsory draft, it could have been predicted that there would not be much cooperation in Bluefields. There, mostly, the army has to "catch" its soldiers.

It is ten in the morning, and I am sitting in the park near the baseball stadium, talking to a friend. Two Australian women are painting a mural with a bunch of kids; other kids are hanging and climbing on the playground equipment. We can hear the cheering from the stadium nearby; there is a doubleheader between the Dantos of Managua and the Costa Atlantica team. It's a hot series. Practically everyone in town is either at the stadium or listening to the game on the radio. Baseball is big in Nicaragua; the U.S. marines introduced it during their occupation.

My friend pokes me and points. Three huge army troop trucks are driving up the road. He knows exactly where they are headed and why.

The trucks stop outside the exits from the stadium, where dozens of food stands are getting ready to sell corn and enchiladas and frescas, fruit and candy and cakes to the between-game crowd. Uniformed troops get off the trucks and circle the stadium. Word travels quickly. In five minutes everyone inside the stadium knows that the army is waiting outside, waiting for the first game to finish and the people to exit. There is no safe way out. The kids who cannot produce proof that they've registered for military service are loaded onto the trucks.

Before the "recruitment" is over, three trucks are filled with kids and driven to the army base.

"It could happen any time, any place," says one young man. "We're afraid to have fun."

They also get picked up in school, which is a policy that undermines the government's efforts to encourage teenagers to stay in school. Some just quit before they turn seventeen.

And there are other boys, from middle-class and wealthy families, who are being sent out of the country to live with relatives in the United States or Costa Rica or Panama or anywhere else they can call on family to help them avoid the draft. They have to leave the country early, though, when they're fourteen or fifteen; if they wait until they're seventeen, the government won't let them out.

Other kids get on buses or walk through the mountains into Honduras or Costa Rica, illegally. If they're caught trying to leave the country, they have to serve time in jail and then their two years in the army.

Of course, there's another side. The volunteers. Francisco is drinking coffee in a restaurant when I meet him. He's wearing his camouflage uniform; his gun is on a chair, and his bulging backpack is on the floor. He responds to my "Buenos días" with a dimpled smile; I ask if I may join him.

"Sure," he says, moving his gun onto the floor so I can sit.

He has a very young face. I ask him how old he is.

"I'll be seventeen next week," he says.

"I guess that means that you went in voluntarily," I say. "How come?"

He tells me that he has only one more month until he's finished with his two-year military service.

"When I turned fifteen," he says, "I started thinking about military service. At first I used to talk about it with my friends once in a while. Then I started thinking about it when I was alone. After a while I was thinking about it all the time. I got to a point where I couldn't think about anything else. I was paralyzed. I mean, really, I couldn't take my mind off it. My head was exploding. So I decided to go voluntarily. I figured, If I do it now, and they don't kill me, I'll be out at seventeen and I won't have to think about it any more. Besides, I knew I had to do it. It's the duty of young people. If we don't defend our country, nobody will."

And then there's Denis, who is walking along the road when we pick him up.

Marco, my taxi driver friend from Managua, is giving four of us foreigners a six-day tour of western Nicaragua: an agricultural adviser from Australia who is working for the government; a woman from Baltimore, here, as I am, to see for herself what's going on; and a school principal—who is also a juggler—from England. We're just coming from a home for deaf-and-dumb children where Juggler (that's what we call him) has given an impromptu show. We just walked in and he started to juggle. The kids flipped. They began to mimic him and laugh and communicate. Juggler can't speak a word of Spanish, but it didn't matter, because his audience couldn't hear. They were talking a special language.

He was a smash success, and they didn't let us leave until they could present us with frescas and crackers topped with honey. Juggler thanked them for the food by giving out balloons, and he closed with a grand finale of flaming torches, flying in the air.

When we leave, Marco drives toward the beach (Nicaragua has wonderful beaches). No one is paying much attention to the scenery when suddenly Juggler screams in English, "Stop!"

Marco, who doesn't speak English, has no trouble understanding. He hits the brakes, and Juggler jumps out and walks toward a soldier who is walking, with his submachine gun over his shoulder, along the side of the road. The gun is nearly the same size as the soldier, who has the stature and the face of a child.

"Come here and ask this kid how old he is," calls Juggler to the woman from Baltimore who has been serving as his translator.

"Twelve" is the answer.

"Are you in the militia?" she asks.

The militia, which protects villages but doesn't go out into the mountains looking for contras, includes people of all ages, from very young to very old.

"Nope," he answers. "I'm in the regular army."

"Ask him if he wants a ride," says Juggler, characteristically frustrated at needing a translator.

Denis climbs in and rests his gun across his and Juggler's legs. In answer to our questions, he tells his story. He used to live in a small border village, the oldest of five kids. One day around six months ago, his parents and one of his sisters were killed by the contras. Denis refused to live with relatives, who had taken in the rest of the kids. All he wanted to do was join the army and avenge the killings.

"But you should be in school," says someone.

"I don't want to be in school. That's what everybody said. Nobody wanted me to join the army. Not even the army wanted me in the army. But I told them that's where I had to be, so they let me in."

They are called "mascots," the young ones, but they're not treated like children. They train, they carry guns, and they go into combat. I would meet three more over the next months, one twelve-year-old and two thirteen-year-olds. One of the thirteen-year-olds was a communications expert. All of them had stories similar to Denis's.

We have only begun asking Denis questions when he tells us we've arrived at his destination. As he climbs out of the car, Juggler gives him a balloon. We turn to wave as we drive off. Denis, in his army uniform, with his submachine gun over his shoulder, is blowing up the balloon.

In the course of my eight months in Nicaragua, I talk to a lot of kids who have volunteered, most of them at sixteen or when they turn seventeen, before they're called up. At first I expect them to tell me that they went in for adventure or to defend the revolution. Some do. But most of them tell me they just wanted to get it over with so they could go on with their schooling and their lives.

Whether they go in voluntarily or wait to get caught, the army experience is pretty much the same for all the *cachorros*. The word means "lion cubs"; that's what the young army men are called. There are T-shirts with baby lions on the front and "I'm your cachorro" written on the back. They're the cubs of Augusto César Sandino, a rebel general who fought to get the U.S. marines out of Nicaragua in the 1920s and 1930s. He was assassinated in 1934 by the first of the ruling Somozas; now he's a hero. His shape, with its cowboy hat and slight hunch, is stenciled on thousands of buildings; it greets arriving tourists on a big billboard at the airport in Managua, also named for him. And the first lesson of the literacy campaign, in which the student learns the vowels, is taught with the sentence, "Sandino, leader of the revolution." *La revolución* contains all five vowels. Sandino is there as a history lesson, and the Sandinistas got their name from Sandino.

It's almost impossible to go anywhere in Nicaragua without seeing uniformed cachorros in olive green or in camouflage. In Managua they're on the buses, in the streets, in your house, in the house next door. They're in troop trucks, they're in jeeps, they're guarding buildings and people. In the other cities they are a noticed presence as well. And near the war zones, they're all over the place. But the majority are in the mountains where nobody sees them. In a country of nearly three and a half million people, more than 65,000 are in the army. Most of them see action. Take Carlos, for example.

Carlos is nineteen. We meet in San Juan del Rio Coco, a town swarming with cachorros who are between stints in the nearby mountains. Everywhere you look there's another "cub" carrying a submachine gun, additional ammunition strapped around his waist, and a backpack behind.

All the backpacks are olive green, but every once in a while I see one with extra pockets and zippers and compartments, made of a better, sturdier fabric. Carlos has one of the better ones.

"Why is your backpack different from the others?" I ask.

"My buddy took it from a dead contra. It's American."

"Did your buddy finish his service?"

"He was killed in battle two months ago."

I ask Carlos to tell me about being a soldier.

"They got me in the street when I was seventeen. I was a kid just hanging out. Nothing mattered too much. Then all of a sudden I was in the army."

"Did you ever consider leaving the country?"

"Nope. I wouldn't leave Nicaragua. It's my country. Those kids who leave, maybe they won't be able to come back."

"So what is it like when you first go in?"

"There's a big change from civilian to military life. At home you have all your friends and family. Then suddenly you don't have anyone. In the mountains nothing's the same as before. In civilian life you're well bathed and clean. In the mountains you live in the same dirty clothes for weeks. It's awful. You feel dirty all the time. Wet and cold and hungry and dirty. And sometimes you can't find water to drink, and all you can think about is how thirsty you are. And you have to put up with animals and mosquitoes.

"You get a lot more aware of things in the mountains. It's very different from reading about it in a book or seeing movies or television. You experience everything directly; you feel suffering in your own flesh. You feel the pain of the mountain.

"What we do is walk. Day and night we walk, looking for contras. We get up in the dark and we walk with our packs, our bullets, our grenades, cans of food, bread, sometimes jam. Sometimes we're carrying seventy pounds. We just keep walking with all that stuff, looking for contras. They don't want to fight with us; what they want to do is destroy cooperatives and blow up fuel tanks and burn down schools. So we go out looking for them. When we find them, they run; so we follow and try to find them again. Eventually they get tired of running from us and they get captured.

"When we get them as prisoners, we try to talk to them and find out who they are. We get a lot of weapons from the captured contras. In my last battle, the one where my buddy got killed, we killed six contras and recovered lots of weapons.

"There are no good times out there. Sometimes you're shooting, and you feel a bullet whiz by your ear. It's scary. One friend of mine was resting, and he didn't know there was a contra five yards away. He was blown up by a hand grenade. They were practically body to body and he never knew it. That's how it is. Even when we're resting, we have to be alert. You always have to be thinking about when the enemy is going to show up.

"Before I was in the service, I used to think that maybe combat would be neat. I found out it's hard. The first time you experience combat, you're really scared; everyone is. A lot of guys get hit the first time out. They stand up. That's how you get killed. You pray and beg God to save you, but you still have to bury your nose in the ground if you're going to save yourself. You've got to think about taking care of yourself and your buddies.

"None of us in my battalion knew each other when we started, but we've really gotten to love each other. We've been through a lot together. We share everything. Everything. Sometimes when it's real calm, we break up into groups, like six or so, and we tell jokes and try to make each other laugh. We try to make it seem as if everything is all right. It makes the day go by. We talk about battles, about getting permissions to go home, about what it would be like to have peace.

"We know that our families are home worrying about us so we send letters; and whenever we can, when we're in a town, we send telegrams [the majority of homes in Nicaragua do not have telephones]. If we have a couple of days in a place where we can have visitors, everybody comes—mothers, brothers, fathers, girlfriends. Even though we become such close friends, we all miss our families. Sometimes when we're walking, especially at night, I think about my girlfriend and what we'd be doing if I were home; and I think about my mother, my brothers, and sisters."

"You told me you were the oldest child in your family. Do you give advice to your brothers and sisters?"

"I've only seen them twice in the last twenty months. But when I do see them I tell them to study hard. That's their responsibility. I'm doing my service so that they can study and live in peace."

"And when it's over for you? What then?"

"I only have four more months to go. I go to bed every night and pray that there won't be any more battles. I have to believe that if I stay alert, everything will come out okay. I'm planning to go back to school when I get out. I need to study for a career, something short like accounting. I used to want to study agriculture, but it takes too long. I've already lost two years.

"I just hope the war doesn't get worse. I mean if the United States puts all its power behind an invasion—like they did in Grenada—well, we'd all have to be fighting again. They're a big power, and we're a small underdeveloped country. It would be absurd to think that we're going to win. But look, we're all ready. If the government calls, we'll be there."

I've run out of questions and begin to thank Carlos for giving me so much of his time and his emotions. He interrupts me.

"You say you're writing a book that will be read by young people in the United States. Can I say something to them in your book?"

"Sure. If I can, I'll use it."

"I'd like to tell them that the contras are trying to destroy our life here in Nicaragua. That their targets are bridges and food and electricity and schools. And that it's mostly us young people who are getting killed. I can't believe that the young people in the United States want to do these things to us. So what I want to say to them is, 'Don't support your government. Demonstrate against Reagan.' "

He pauses and looks at me reflectively. "Will it really be in a book?"

I nod. "Probably."

"Maybe if young people could have more power in the United States, there wouldn't be this war."

"Brainwashed. All the kids are brainwashed, especially the cachorros. The Sandinistas get them in the army for two years and they brainwash them. It's the Sandinistas, not the contras, who have taken away our freedom and made such a mess of this country."

That is the man's answer when I read him Carlos's message to young people in the States. I don't know the man's name, but he is driving a new Toyota Land Cruiser and he has picked up a hitchhiker—me.

The driver is a man in his late thirties, dressed in a smart-looking plaid shirt and gray corduroy pants. Like most people who discover that I am writing a book, he wants to tell me what he thinks.

He does not volunteer his name; I don't ask. I have found that casually met people tend to tell you more if you don't know their names.

The man works for the government, he tells me, which is why he has the use of the Land Cruiser. As an agronomist, he has one of the most important professions in this agricultural country. He tells me that he is the director of an entire section of the country for the major government-based agricultural organization. It is a high-level position with the Sandinista government. On our trip he stops in two local offices of this organization while I tag along. It appears that he has told me the truth about his job.

"The Sandinistas," he volunteers, "have made a mess of this country. There's a shortage of everything. You have to stand in line for meat or sugar or beans or milk, unless you buy them on the black market. And the average Nicaraguan doesn't have the money for the black market. And as for manufactured things, forget it. A window breaks, there is no glass; a car needs a part, you can't buy it. You can't even buy toilet paper. The Sandinistas talk about dignity. Where is dignity when you can't even have toilet paper in your bathroom?"

Most of the people I meet who are angry at the Sandinistas are angry because of shortages—of food, of fuel, of water, of soap, of shampoo, of makeup, of medical supplies, of spare parts, of toys, of construction materials—of practically everything.

No hay (pronounced "eye"), "there isn't any," is perhaps the most frequently used phrase in the country. You just don't walk into a store in Nicaragua and say, "May I have. . . ." You ask, "Is there?" It goes like this:

"Hay Pepsi?"

"No hay."

"Hay pan [bread]?"

"No hay."

"Hay fósforos [matches]?"

"No hay."

"Hay jabón [soap]?"

"No hay."

"Hay leche [milk]?"

"No hay."

"Hay pasta de dientes [toothpaste]?"

"No hay."

And so on.

"But worst of all," continues the man in the car, "is the shortage of freedom. I work for the government. I'd lose my job if I ever talked this way to my colleagues. People are thrown in jail for criticizing the Sandinistas. They've closed down the only newspaper that was critical. And television is *Sandinista* television.

"They say there's pluralism [a many-party political system], but those other parties are nothing but puppets. We don't live in Nicaragua, we live in Sandinista-land. The army is the Popular Sandinista Army; we sing the Sandinista hymn; the schoolbooks teach the Sandinista version of history. The FSLN is supposed to be a party, but it's *become* Nicaragua. Do you think the Sandinistas would let anyone else win an election?

"It was that way with Somoza too. It's the same tortilla, just the other side."

The car comes to a stop. A herd of maybe a hundred cattle is walking toward us. A minute earlier we passed a boy on horseback, waving a red flag. The driver honks his horn and moves through the herd. The cattle are slow to get out of the way. Three more times in our trip we plow our way through herds of cattle. It's the main source of income in this part of the country.

"Talk to some of these cattlemen," he says. "Ask them what the Sandinistas have done for them. They [the Sandinistas] have taken control of everything. They control prices and exports and banks and land use. They're trying to control our minds, too."

It all came out at me in a rush of words, as though he had been saving it for years and finally had a chance to speak.

"Has nothing good come from the revolution?" I ask.

"The literacy crusade was good from the point of view that they taught the campesinos to read, but the Sandinistas used it to indoctrinate the campesinos, to teach them how wonderful the Sandinistas are. And the health campaign has probably saved a lot of lives. But what's the price of freedom?"

I ask him about his family, especially his parents.

"They left the country in 1979, and the Sandinistas confiscated their land. It's a cooperative now."

"And you? Are you planning to leave?"

"It's my country. I won't let them drive me out."

"What do you think about the contras?"

"They're a bunch of thugs."

When I climb out of the car, my head is spinning. There are so many people in Nicaragua who are hurting. Sometimes in a matter of minutes I hear first one side and then the other side. And I can empathize with both. And I want to holler, but I don't know who to holler at. "Why can't these people live in peace, with dignity?" I want to shout. But who would listen?

For the entire time I am in Nicaragua, I never stop asking people what they think of their government, what they think of the contras. Whenever I feel I have a sense of what the Nicaraguan people really think, something happens and I realize that I don't know at all.

One night, in a restaurant in Rivas, a town near the Costa Rican border, I find myself sitting at a table next to two men in their early sixties. I am sitting alone, and they ask me what I am doing in Nicaragua. One of the men is an engineer; the other is a lawyer and the owner of a hotel.

"We've been friends since we were kids," says the engineer. "And today we're still friends, even though we're on opposite sides. He's a reactionary [against the government], and I'm a staunch Sandinista."

The lawyer excuses himself to go to the bathroom. While he is gone, I ask the engineer, the Sandinista, to give me an idea of what percentage of the Nicaraguans are against the government.

He thinks a minute. "Oh," he says. "About two percent."

Minutes later the lawyer returns and the engineer

excuses himself. I ask the lawyer, who is against the government himself, the same question.

"What percent of the people do you think are against the Sandinistas?"

"Ninety percent," he replies.

There is only one theme that remains fairly constant. Hardly anyone likes the contras.

Only one woman openly admitted to me that she hated the government so much she wanted the contras to win. "I hope they drop the atom bomb on the Sandinistas," she said.

I wondered how the bomb would know who was who.

12

ANOTHER KIND OF WAR

he war. You can never forget it. Even in the cities.

Not because of the bombs or the mines. Most urban Nicaraguans never hear them.

Not because of the sound of shooting in the streets or the sight of marching troops. That's what I thought war would be like. But it isn't. Not this war. There is no shooting in the streets, and except for special parades, you never see marching troops.

The war that the United States is sponsoring in Nicaragua is a different kind of war. The U.S. strategists call it "low-intensity conflict." That means that they aren't trying to win this war by killing a lot of people (although they do advise killing "certain" people like teachers and Sandinista leaders). Instead, they hope to do it through economic, psychological, and political "warfare." There is a carefully planned logic to this new kind of war. It goes like this:

1. The U.S. goal is to get the Sandinistas out of power. To do it, they need the support of the Nicaraguan people.
2. The success of the revolution and the early programs of the Sandinistas created a pride and a strong nationalistic feeling among most Nicaraguans. If the Sandinistas do a good job, if the people are happy, the people won't have any reason to want to get rid of their government.
3. So the trick is to get the people angry at the Sandinistas. The best way to do that is to stop the government from doing good things for the people. And to try to make the people miserable.

Nicaragua is a poor country to begin with. Even in the best of times, there is barely enough food to feed the people. And the country has to import most manufactured products—like machines and medicines, tools and toys. The money Nicaragua earns from its exports—primarily coffee, cotton, shellfish, bananas, and sugar—is small compared to the amount it spends on imports.

Add to that the costs of a war, and the country is in serious trouble. Soldiers need guns and clothes and helicopters and tanks. They have to eat and train and be transported from place to place. That doesn't leave much for literacy and health programs, for improvements of living conditions, for the social, cultural and educational programs that the Sandinistas promised their people.

But the most devastating effect of the war is the scarcity of food. A lot of those soldiers, if there were no war, would be farming, growing food to feed the people. Instead, they have to be fed themselves.

And there are thousands of acres of good farmland in the war zones that have been abandoned both for safety and defense reasons. Instead of growing food, the fields are growing weeds.

Contributing to the scarcity of food is the fact that the contras are trying directly to reduce the food supply in the country. Some of their prime targets are food storage tanks, tractors, other farm equipment, vehicles that transport food, and even fields of crops ready to be harvested.

If people don't have enough food, they're bound to get angry. A lot of them already are. When I ask about life in Nicaragua, nearly everyone begins with the facts that there isn't enough food and that what there is costs too much.

A fifteen-year-old boy whose mother works as a laundress for a middle-class family tells me, "My mother is angry all the time. She hardly ever laughs any more. She says it's because she can't feed her family; and I know that's true because half the time we don't have enough rice and beans, and we hardly ever have meat. And there isn't enough milk for the baby. She always complains how expensive everything is. She can't buy us shoes or pants. She says it was better before the revolution, that the Sandinistas have ruined the country. She isn't the same any more. I think maybe she's a little crazy."

There isn't enough food, and what there is is too expensive. There aren't enough *things* either. Nicaragua used to get most of its manufactured goods from the United States. Then, in 1985 and 1986, the U.S. government declared a trade embargo—no more trading with Nicaragua. No more U.S. toothpaste or shampoo or nail polish or ketchup. No more Levi's or Adidas or U.S. blenders. No glasses or pots, no radios or tape decks. No more parts to fix the U.S. cars or the U.S. water pumps or the U.S. tractors or the U.S. sewing machines.

"I can hardly remember what it was like when you could get anything you wanted," says Rosa, the twelve-year-old girl who had asked me for a chocolate bar and an apple for Christmas. "My grandmother says the supermarkets used to be filled with things. I remember when she used to bring us corn flakes and raisins and bubble gum. And I used to have toys from the United States, and a doll."

I visit a sewing cooperative one day. All the tailors are disabled people, in wheelchairs, on crutches, handicapped in some way. One of the men tells me he had been a bum until the Sandinistas came along and taught him how to earn a living by sewing. Others nod their heads while they listen to him. He and the others are now a part of a group that makes clothes. Although handicapped, they are useful members of society. There are twelve of them. The only problem is that five of their twelve U.S.–made machines aren't working, and there are no parts to fix them.

Nicaragua has turned into a country of "no hay"; you name it, there isn't any.

No one likes to stand in line or to do without. The Sandinistas keep telling the people that the problems of scarcity, both food and things, are "por la agresión," (because of the aggression, because of the war). It's por la agresión that people have to stand in lines to get their rationed food. It's por la agresión that they have to pay hundreds of times more for a tomato than they did in the old days. It's por la agresión that the supermarket shelves are empty. And it's por la agresión that there's such a thriving black market.

According to the Sandinistas, it's por la agresión that

the buses are so horrible, that the telephone service is bad, that the roads have holes in them.

The people are getting tired of not having anything. They're getting tired of standing in lines. And they're getting tired of being told that everything that is going wrong in the country is por la agresión.

Por la agresión has become a joke. A lot of people don't believe it anymore. Even the FSLN newspaper has a cartoon one day that pictures a woman serving her husband a badly burned dinner. He is looking up at her with a "what's this?" look on his face; and she is saying, "Por la agresión."

Everything that's wrong in Nicaragua isn't because of the war. People know that the Sandinistas have bungled. Everyone you meet has a story: about a boatload of desperately needed medicines stuck so long in the port of Corinto that the medicines go out of date and have to be dumped; or about the dozens of tractors that are driven off the ship without oil and are ruined before they get to their destinations; or about the thirty minibuses that arrive in Managua from East Germany and inside of a few months, twenty-two of them are unusable; the drivers, all recently demobilized soldiers, have crashed or ruined them.

There is also corruption in the government. Everyone knows that corruption, so long a part of Nicaragua's history, didn't disappear one day in 1979.

So, clearly, it isn't *all* por la agresión as the Sandinistas would like everyone to believe. But, just as clearly, the aggression *is* causing much of the suffering. And people are grumbling. Many of those who have money saved up are standing in line at the U.S. Embassy, trying to get permission to go north. But most don't have any choice; they stay and learn to adjust or continue the fight.

"Are we going to give up because of hunger?" asks Daniel Ortega at a mass rally. "No!" shouts the crowd.

During one of my visits with a family in the town of Estelí, I am helping some friends prepare a chicken dinner for a victorious little league baseball team. We are dunking just-killed chickens into boiling water so that we can pull the feathers out. One of the women is having a hard time.

"This old bird is a lot like us," she says. "They'll have to pull mighty hard at our feathers before they get *us* to give in."

At times, however, it appears that the U.S. strategy is winning. People *are* suffering and they often tell me how angry they are at the Sandinistas. But a few questions later it becomes apparent that, while they may be angry at their government, most of them do not support the contras.

The fact is that the contras are killing Nicaraguan boys, and every family knows someone who has died. There is one week I go, with the family I am visiting, to the funerals of three young soldiers. The fifteen-year-old daughter in this family, who spends her life listening to a rock music station and flirting with cachorros, is going off early one Sunday morning with some girlfriends.

"Where are you going?" I ask her.

"First we're going por allá to buy some flowers." She gestures. "And then we're going to the cemetery. Every Sunday we go and put flowers on the graves of boys we know." However hungry they may be, however angry at the Sandinistas, there are few Nicaraguans who can support the U.S.-backed contras who are killing their sons, their brothers, their boyfriends.

One of the other ways that the contras are trying to win over the Nicaraguan people is through "political warfare." In the border areas the contras have dropped leaflets into campesino villages, and radio programs that come from Honduras and Costa Rica are designed to incite the campesinos to turn against the Sandinistas. "The Sandinistas are communists," say the messages. "They are spending the Nicaraguan treasury on bullets instead of food." "They are atheists, and they won't allow you to go to church." "They are terrorists, and they are forcing your children into a totalitarian, Marxist draft."

There was also a newspaper, *La Prensa*, the most popular in Nicaragua, that was consistently critical of the Sandinistas. Many people say that the newspaper was receiving money from the CIA to write things against the government. In 1986 the Sandinistas closed down the paper, justifying their action with the argument that a country at war cannot permit the enemy to have such easy access to the people.

Closing down the newspaper and censoring the others are probably the most controversial actions the Sandinistas have taken. Freedom of the press is considered a sacred right in the democratic world. The Nicaraguan constitution guarantees that freedom.

Because of the war, say the Sandinistas, certain freedoms have to be suspended. They say that they cannot allow the enemy to flourish in their midst. Using the same argument, the Sandinistas have jailed people on suspicion of collaborating with the enemy and moved entire villages, against their will, to "safer" places.

When questioned about this, the Sandinista answer is that the suspension of freedoms has historically been one of the necessary facts of war in all countries. And, they always add, the war to overthrow the government is not a war that they want; it is a war that is being kept alive by the United States.

In August of 1987 Ortega and the presidents of Costa Rica, Guatemala, El Salvador, and Honduras agreed to a plan for peace in Central America. According to the plan, there was to be a regional cease-fire by November 5. Later the date was extended to January 5, 1988.

All the countries agreed to the conditions of the plan. Additionally, all the signers of the plan agreed to enact democratic reforms, including guarantees of a free press, free elections, and amnesty for guerrilla groups.

As part of the plan, outside countries were prohibited from sending military aid to guerrilla troops. In Nicaragua's case, this meant that the United States could no longer support the contras.

Ortega acted to comply with the plan. His government allowed *La Prensa* to resume publishing. It offered amnesty to the contras. Elections, promised Ortega, would be held as scheduled. "If the people of Nicaragua, through their votes, say that we (the Sandinistas) should not be in office, then we'd be willing to give up office," he told reporters.

"The Sandinistas are simply not going to give up power," said one U.S. official. "Anyone who believes that is fooling himself."

Reagan said that he could not support the peace plan, that it did not go far enough. And besides, he did not trust the Sandinistas, no matter what they said or did. While the Central American countries were working toward peace, Reagan was asking for an additional $270 million in aid for the contras.

"I make a solemn vow," Reagan said in October. "As long as there is breath in this body, I will speak and work, strive and struggle, for the cause of the Nicaraguan freedom fighters [contras]."

Said Ortega, "The reply of the United States has been to try to wrest away from our hard-won liberty and to send Somoza's Guardia [the contras] back to Nicaragua to rule."

It would be months, perhaps years, before the final results of the peace plan could be assessed. The question, the big question in many people's minds, was, What would happen in Nicaragua if there were no war? Would there still be lines? Would there still be a draft? Would there be freedom of the press?

No one really knows. Not until the war goes away.

13

A STUDY
IN CONTRASTS

s I move through Nicaragua, constantly aware of its violent past and living on a day-to-day basis with its violent present, there are times when I think I might explode from the intensity. Intensity and anguish that come from ever-present death, from the difficulties of everyday life, from trying to make sense out of the different stories I'm hearing, and from my own feelings of anger about the role the United States is playing in all this.

I suddenly find myself staying away from foreigners, most of whom want to talk politics all the time. I find myself laughing louder than usual and sometimes inappropriately. And I discover that I am asking fewer questions about the war and more about what young people in Nicaragua do for fun.

Yes, there *is* more to Nicaragua than politics and problems. Discos, for example.

There are discos in Managua with names like Wolfman Jack, Infinito, Pink Panther, Tom Cat. Slick, air-conditioned discos with velvety booths, real glasses, and multifaceted mirrored balls and strobes that splash sun and flash colors on shimmering bodies in stylish clothes. Sergio Valenti. Calvin Klein. Leather pants. Hip belts. Nike sneakers. Spike heels.

Discos where you can hear Springsteen, Madonna, Mick Jagger, Janet Jackson. Most of the discos play almost exclusively American rock, with a few Spanish ballads and some salsa thrown in.

The girls in the fancy discos, dressed as though they had stepped out of a U.S. fashion magazine, are part of that comfortable middle class. They're called *chicas plásticas*, "plastic chicks." For the most part they are the sons and daughters of people who have money, though they are not necessarily rich. They are the children of businesspeople, government officials, professionals, black marketeers, foreign diplomats, technicians. Some of the people in the discos work, often with private companies who pay better than the government; others go to school. Still others do both. There are also a significant number of internationals at the fancy discos, mostly from Europe, the United States, Canada, and Australia.

But dancing isn't reserved for people with money. In Managua there are lots of places to dance, from grubby clubs to giant tents. What they all seem to share is American rock music.

"Doesn't it seem strange to you that your music is

the music of the enemy?" I ask a young man after we finish dancing.

"Not a bit. The United States produces good things. We're not savages. We like good things too. We like your music, your clothes, your movies, your television programs, your machines." Tina Turner is belting one out in the background as he talks.

There are discos in the war-zone towns as well. Sandra's is a giant, open room with a raised platform surrounding a huge dance floor. A solid violet light shines into the middle of the dance floor and flashing yellow, green, and red bulbs are spotted around the room. The place is packed with kids; "twelve and up," says the young woman who is selling tickets.

Jalapa, the town I'm in, is fairly close to the border and has been the site of numerous attacks. Sometimes people can lie in their beds at night and listen to the guns and the bombs in the surrounding hills. The town is filled with young Sandinista soldiers—and so is Sandra's.

"When you have a war, you have to enjoy yourself too. The two things go together," says one young soldier wearing a New York Yankees baseball cap.

Some of the guys are wearing their uniforms; most are not. There's a rule that says no one in uniform can drink. So the cachorros put on their civilian clothes: jeans; pants of various colors; T-shirts, some of the sleeves rolled up to the shoulder; cotton short-sleeved shirts. Many of the young men are still in their heavy combat boots, hopping around on the dance floor. And there is a smattering of military hats.

"Don't you want somebody to love? Don't you need somebody to love?" Jefferson Airplane is filling the room. Three guys in a row come over to ask a pretty girl to dance. She is wearing a white skirt, blue blouse tucked in, and a wide black belt. Flats and white socks. She is leaning seductively against the railing, talking to two girlfriends. Without even a polite smile, she says no to each of the dance offers. The first two walk away, accepting their fate. The third begs a little.

"Come on," he says, taking her hand and trying to pull her onto the dance floor. She shakes her head. "Come on," he repeats.

But there are more guys than girls in the room, and she knows she has a choice. I watch her as she looks around. Finally her eyes stop at a young man standing with two other boys about ten feet away. She stares until he looks over. Then she smiles and nods. He walks over.

"Don't you want somebody to love?"

After each song the boys walk back to join their buddies and the girls return to the girls. And the rite begins again.

"The girls in the war zones have all the guys," says a fourteen-year-old Managua girl when I tell her about Sandra's. "All the older boys in our school are gone, and we're not so interested in the ones who are our age."

Her best friend interrupts. "But next week all the guys who went in two years ago are coming home. We can't wait. When they left we were too young for them, but we're not any more."

"We're always thinking about the boys in the military. What are they doing? Are they safe? You know, they could get killed. We think about them all the time.

"One of our classmates left the country a few months ago to live with relatives in the United States. We don't think about him any more; he's run out on his military service. We think a lot more about the boys who are risking their lives for the revolution."

The girls are spending the afternoon together, planning what to wear to a fifteenth birthday party that night. In Nicaragua, fifteen is the big one, not sixteen. There is going to be a mobile disco and food and, regrettably, mostly boys their own age. But in two weeks, just fourteen days, a whole new crop of older boys will arrive from the mountains. The girls are already planning what to wear when they meet the buses.

It is dusk. The western sky casts a pink hue over the town of Estelí. I am walking down the street, and I smile at an approaching woman who is in her mid-sixties. Suddenly, though I have never seen her before, she throws her arms around me and says, "Thank you for coming to our country."

The next night I'm at a high school dance. On the loudspeaker, Michael Jackson is singing, and the kids are crowded onto the center of the dance floor, which is really the outdoor basketball court between two classroom buildings. There's an especially festive air about the night. It's the first dance in months. They used to have them all the time, but people can't afford the admission price anymore.

At the far end of the court, where the little brothers and sisters are playing tag, there's a booth where beer is sold. Very few of the teenagers are drinking; the beer is expensive.

I am standing at the edge of the dance floor when a drunken man approaches me. He is about the same age as the woman who had hugged me the day before.

"Where are you from?" he asks.

"The United States."

He lifts his white shirt, which he is wearing out, over his pants, and shows me a hand grenade that is tucked into the waistband.

"You know what I want to do with this?" he says, fingering the grenade. "I want to shove it in Reagan's mouth."

Love and hate. Life and death. Laughter and tears. A dream of peace, a reality of violence. Nicaragua is a land of emotional extremes. The symbol of the national women's organization is a photograph of a woman in an army uniform with a gun over her shoulder and a nursing baby at her breast.

This is a passionate country, and so much of the passion is created by the tension between extremes. Even the landscape creates tension.

One day, three friends and I drive with Marco to Grenada, a city on the northwest side of Lake Nicaragua. The lake is huge, 3,000 square miles, larger than any lake in the United States, more than twice the size of Rhode Island. The northwest corner of the lake, where we take a boat trip, is filled with tiny, picturesque islands formed by ancient volcanic activity.

We wave to families picnicking on the islands as we work our way to a peaceful spot where we can dive into the water and enjoy the serenity of the setting. The water is calm and cool; soon, we foreigners are the only people in sight.

Later, when we return to the car, Marco, who was not on the boat with us, tells us that the same volcanic activity that centuries ago created the islands also cut off this water—and all its forms of life—from the Pacific Ocean. It is the only freshwater lake in the world that contains sharks!

Marco laughs his deep resounding belly laugh as we react to the news that we have been swimming with sharks.

"Want to see the volcano?" says Marco when we are on the road again. "It's alive."

"Sure."

He drives on. "The gases from the volcano have rotted all these houses," he tells us as we get closer. "And you can't grow anything here either."

We can see the smoke in the distance as we wind up the mountain. When we get to the top, Marco stops. "Por allá," he points as he turns off the motor. He needn't have pointed. The top of this mountain is spewing out ominous gray smoke about twenty yards from the car.

We climb a short hill and stand at the edge of a crater perhaps a hundred yards in diameter. No one speaks as we look down into a deep, gaping hole, a roaring gaping hole that is belching smoke from its bowels. The sound is unearthly—it is a wailing, a hissing, a roaring that is eerily coming from the center of the earth, a hot, boiling inferno.

No one can speak; we are all enveloped in our own fear. It is as though we are touching something profoundly spiritual, something, perhaps, we are not meant to touch or, perhaps, something that contains a cosmic message we are meant to decipher.

After about a half an hour, we walk to the car silently, and Marco drives to the other side of the crater. There are steps leading to the peak of the mountain, from which you can see the view in all directions. There are two teenage couples ahead of us on the stairs, Nicaraguan youths about sixteen and seventeen. The boys are dressed in jeans and T-shirts, the girls in tight pants and over-sized shirts, nearly down to their knees. They are holding hands, each couple, and pulling and teasing and racing each other up the steps. As we begin our climb, we can hear their squeals and laughter ahead of us. And we can see them as they stand on the platform, arm in arm.

By the time we reach the top, they have begun their descent. Seconds after we pass each other, the wind suddenly changes direction, and the poisonous gases, which had been going straight up, blow directly at the bottom of the stairs, directly at the two couples. There are screams, coughs, groans. Some of the gas comes in our direction. It burns my eyes, my throat. I am choking. I am in pain. I hold my breath and close my eyes. From down below I can hear wailing sounds from the kids.

Then, just as suddenly as it came, the gas moves off in a different direction. In minutes, the pain is over. We race down the stairs and join Marco, who is waiting for us near the car.

"They're lucky," he says as the kids begin to regain their breath. "The Guardia used to toss people their age out of helicopters right into the middle."

His loud, hoarse, hearty laughter competes with the roaring volcano.

Then, without speaking, Marco gestures toward the side of the crater. Hundreds of little green parrots are moving in and out of the cracks; and hundreds more are fluttering around and resting on some trees at the crest. The birds are sporting that iridescent green that has been mastered only by parrots; the trees are lush with foliage. Somehow they have learned to thrive amid the deadly gases and the constant roar from the black hole. Somehow they've been able to work it out, the birds and the trees, so they can all coexist on this little, flawed piece of earth.

THE QUESTION AGAIN

There is a family party, my real family, and I am flying to Florida to attend. Marco—with three of his kids in the car—is driving me to the airport.

Tonight Ramón is going to someone's fifteenth birthday party. He is fighting with his father over a pair of new sneakers that fits both of them. Ramón wants to wear them to the party; Marco has them on his feet.

As I walk out the door, Juan Carlos is standing on the dining room table. "Te vas a caer!" You're going to fall! screams his grandmother, rescuing him and carrying him out to the porch to wave good-bye.

As we are getting into the car, the seven-year-old drags me off to see a dead, dried-up lizard he has discovered in the woodpile.

I am carrying a set of carved wooden wine goblets as a gift from Ramón's mother to my mother.

I have a ripe mango in my purse, a going-away present from one of the kids.

I am also carrying an empty duffel bag which I will fill, before I come back, with used clothing and cast-off shoes.

As usual, the daily papers are reporting death at the hands of the "Yankee aggressor." But as I ride to the airport, it is not the aggressor that I am thinking about. My search for villains has been overshadowed by Ramón and Celina, by Marco and Evenor, by Juan Carlos and Elena; by the mothers, the fathers, the daughters, the sons—the people—the victims.

The flight is quick. Miami is closer to Nicaragua than it is to New York.

My family is curious.

"Nicaragua? Isn't it dangerous? Don't they hate you for being an American?" asks an uncle.

"What are they like? How do they live?" asks a sixteen-year-old cousin. "I mean, is it, like, primitive? Like tribes." She is embarrassed not to know.

"Oh, wait a minute," says her sister. "We studied those countries in my Spanish class. Is Nicaragua the one where the good government is fighting the bad guerrillas? Or is it the one where the bad government is fighting the good guerrillas?"

Depends who you ask.

ACKNOWL-
EDGMENTS

My warmest thanks to Doña
Juana García and Franci Dormus, who shared their homes,
their families, their secrets, and who offered their shoulders when I needed them.

To the people all over Nicaragua whose rockers I
rocked in, whose beds and cots and hammocks I slept in,
and who shared with me their food when there was barely
enough for themselves. And to the many who talked with
me in restaurants, on buses, in parks, in schools, at the
beaches.

A special thanks to the young people, who were always ready to talk. Even though I have changed their

names, Ramón, whose friendship I treasured; his parents, Marco and Teresa; and the others—Carlos, Elena, Maria, and Mario—are real people. Without their honesty and openness, this book could not have been written.

To Evenor, whose story of his literacy crusade is, for me, the most meaningful part of the book.

To Mariko and Reina, who got me through the bureaucracy so that I could meet the people.

To Yadira Ortiz, who trusted me with her library.

To Bob and Elaine Friedman, who provided the nurturing, the refrigerator, and an invaluable sounding board, even though they didn't always agree.

To Frank Sloan, whose idea it was; and who stuck with me through a multitude of distress calls from Managua, from Estelí, and from Massachusetts, Connecticut, and Florida. Without his editorial guidance and his friendship, it would never have happened.

And especially to my children, Jan and Mitch, who kept me going with their encouragement, their support, and their love. I know it wasn't easy. My thanks, my gratitude, and my love.

GLOSSARY

Aquí, allá,
  el Yanqui morirá
	Here, there,
	  the Yankee will die

brigadista	member of a brigade
buenos días	good morning
buenas tardes	good afternoon
cachorro	lion cub; in this context, young soldier
campesino	peasant farmer
campo	farm country
¿Cómo se llama usted?	What is your name?

compañero	companion, friend; a friendly way of addressing a fellow revolutionary
contra	short for *contrarevolucionario*: refers to the U.S.–supported army that is fighting the government of Nicaragua
contrarevolucionario	someone who is against the revolution
en punto	on the dot, referring to time
escoba	broom
fresca	a sweetened fruit drink
FSLN	Frente Sandinista de Liberación Nacional; National Sandinista Liberation Front; the official name of the Sandinista party.
gallo pinto	a mixture of fried rice and beans; a Nicaraguan staple
Guardia	short for Guardia Nacional, the National Guard, Somoza's army
guerrillas	members of an irregular force who are fighting to overthrow the existing government of a country
hay; ¿hay?	there is; is there?
Hay que cumplir	One must fulfill one's obligation
la revolución	the revolution

mango	a tropical fruit
maní	peanut
me llamo	my name is
mercado	market
muchachos	kids; refers to the young guerrilla fighters in the revolution
muchachos locos	crazy kids
nacatamal	a stuffed dumpling wrapped in a banana leaf
no hay	there isn't any
novela	soap opera
oreja	ear; in this context, spy
otra vez	another time; again
por allá	over there
¡Patria libre o morir!	Free country or die
piri	short for rabid dog; contra slang for Sandinista
por la agresión	because of the war
Purísima	December holiday honoring the Virgin Mary
¡Qué barbaridad el transporte!	How horrendous this transportation is!
¡Que le vaya bien!	May it go well for you; loosely, have a good time
señora	Mrs.; lady
Te vo⁓ ⁊ caer	You are going to fall

SUGGESTED READING

Cabezas, Omar. *Fire from the Mountain: The Making of a Sandinista*. New York: Crown Publishers, 1985 (also paperback. New York: New American Library, 1986).

    A first-person account of how the author survived as a Sandinista guerrilla in the mountains. Written with humor, honesty, and gusto.

Collins, Joseph. *What Difference Could a Revolution Make? Food and Farming in the New Nicaragua*. San Francisco: Institute for Food and Development Policy, 1983.

    A simple explanation of the food problems in a poor agrarian country and a look at how the Sandinistas dealt with them in the first two years after the revolution; interviews with people about their experiences in those early years and their expectations for the future.

Davis, Peter. *Where Is Nicaragua?* New York: Simon & Schuster, 1987.
Interesting for the questions the author asks and for the doubts he raises. The author talks with Sandinista officials, opposing political leaders, businessmen, U.S. government officials, and people who frequent the Intercontinental Hotel in Managua.

Dickey, Christopher. *With the Contras: A Reporter in the Wilds of Nicaragua.* New York: Simon & Schuster, 1986.
A *Washington Post* reporter writes graphically about his travels with the contras. This highly readable book will shock anyone who views the contras as fighters for freedom.

Levie, Alvin. *Nicaragua: The People Speak.* South Hadley, Massachusetts: Bergin & Garvey Publishers, 1985.
1984 interviews with people from all over Nicaragua and from all walks of life. This is a human book, but 1984 is a long time ago and the interviews must be read as history rather than news.

Meiselas, Susan. *Nicaragua.* New York: Pantheon Books, 1981.
A book of photographs documenting the Nicaraguan revolution. Adds a visual dimension to an understanding of the country and its people.

Miller, Valerie. *Between Struggle and Hope: The Nicaraguan Literacy Campaign.* Boulder, Colorado: Westview Press, 1985.
A well-written, well-researched, dynamic book. The author was there from the idea of the campaign to the appraisal of it. The chapter titled, "The Campaign in Operation" will bring tears to your eyes.

Randall, Margaret. *Sandino's Daughters*. Trumansburg, N.Y.: Crossing Press, 1981.

> This controversial author, a longtime supporter of both the Cuban and Nicaraguan revolutions, has interviewed women who participated in the revolution and in some cases, their mothers as well. Their stories present personal recollections of the fight to overthrow Somoza.

Rosset, Peter, and John Vandermeer, eds. *The Nicaragua Reader: Documents of a Revolution under Fire*. New York: Grove Press, 1983.

> An anthology of speeches, articles, and excerpts from books that presents the history, the problems, the controversy of Nicaragua through 1983. A good overview of the early years and a presentation of the Reagan position in his and his advisers' words.

INDEX

ABOUT THE AUTHOR

Rita Golden Gelman, author of more than sixty books for young people, lived in Central America for nearly two years. Eight months of this time was spent in Nicaragua. She has a master's degree in anthropology from UCLA and a B.A. in English literature from Brandeis. She grew up in Bridgeport, Connecticut, and has lived in New York and Los Angeles.